Life Skills
For Tween Girls

A Glow Up, Self-Love Survival Guide to Become THAT
Girl, Crush Anxiety, Master Money, Achieve Goals, &
Discover What Most Adults Wish They Knew!

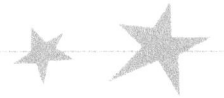

Aniela Publications

Table of Contents

INTRODUCTION

Hey Bestie, While Everyone Else Is Figuring Out How to Grow Up, Are You Ready to Glow Up?

Hey girlie! Grab a cup because I'm about to spill the tea on a lot of things, so put up your feet and get cozy; we're gonna get straight to it. I hope you are ready for some reading and reflecting—maybe even some practical application of the life-changing lessons you're about to learn. These are some essential life skills that you're going to want to reference often because they will benefit you for the rest of your life.

Each chapter of this book addresses a different essential topic—each revealing secrets that will provide you with life skills to make you the CEO of your tween life. These secrets will help you step into your teenage years with confidence. Changes with your body, the tools to help you achieve your goals, handling money like a boss, dopamine decor, handling bullies? Physically, mentally, financially, and spiritually, I've got you covered!

I will cover questions you may have had on your mind but weren't sure how to find answers to, or maybe you felt too shy or uncomfortable to ask. Instead, you were wondering about the changes in your body and keeping it low-key because you didn't know if anyone else was going through similar things. Or, you could have been wondering how to transform your bedroom just like how you're transforming from being a kid to a teenager so it could glow up like you.

While you're enjoying the final years of middle school, you're probably realizing that you are going from being the oldest in your school to starting from scratch as a freshman at your new high school. It may feel a little scary, but it's also an exciting new time where you get a fresh new start!

Instead of having to prove yourself all over again, you would just like to have answers to some of the questions on your mind. Then, instead of trying to fake it, you could enter the new school year with confidence and be the one dishing out the advice to your friends. Right now, though, you need a guide that is going to do more than calm your nerves—a guide that will help you slay at things like having great friendships, being fit, being confident, exuding self-confidence, and saving for the future.

To prepare for the next stage in life, you are about to discover some life hacks that few people know or will tell you about. For real, there is a LOT of information in this book that you will find insanely helpful!

I hope you're amped because I most definitely am!

CHAPTER ONE

Self-Love Life Skills

The Most Essential Power is Loving Every Ounce of You and Knowing You're Good Enough!

A successful life is built on a foundation of self-love. Approaching the world from a perspective of self-love makes building your dream life easier to do. This is because self-love is the most important skill you will need throughout your years. The ability to love and accept yourself fully, at all times, and without judgment is like adding fertilizer to the soil that nourishes the tree of your life. It will help you to continuously make beneficial decisions. Once you have learned how to love yourself and what it means to apply self-love throughout your life, you will move through the world differently. You will find that instead of sabotaging your efforts, you will make choices that lead to your ultimate success.

Self-sabotage isn't something that anybody sets out to do on purpose. It happens as a result of subconscious beliefs. These are beliefs that you may not even realize you have. They became a part of your personality slowly over time. Maybe someone told you that your dreams were a waste of time or unrealistic. Or maybe someone's mean comment about how you played violin in orchestra made you feel like you wanted to quit and change electives. When you first heard these words that did not benefit you, you may have believed them without question. You did this because the words probably came from somebody you trusted. You allowed these words to become a part of who you are to the point of believing in them yourself. Listening to these words time and time again via the voice in your head can hold you back from your true happiness.

Their daily impact seems insignificant, yet over time, the effect builds up. For example, you may fall asleep at your desk instead of studying for an upcoming test. This could stem from the belief that your efforts are not worthwhile. Or, you may "forget" to pack your gym outfit on the day of tryouts. You might do this because you secretly believe that you will not succeed. These and other small actions can add up over time. These mistakes will slowly take your life in a direction that is different from the one you had planned. You could end up failing the semester or even the school year. You may miss out on opportunities to travel with the team because, if you would have packed your kit, you would definitely have succeeded in the tryouts.

Maybe events could have worked out differently if you had somebody who was constantly with you, someone who could remind you to set your alarm or double-check that you had packed everything you needed—somebody who had all the time in the world to just love on you and remind you to do the little things that could lead to your success. Instead, you end up making small mistakes that take you to places that are not on your personal road map.

Let's Start With Positive Self-Talk

Somebody who loves you wants the best for you. They give advice that helps you make the best decisions. But wait a minute, there is somebody who is constantly with you. This person talks to you all the time, and you listen to them, but you might not always follow the advice they give.

As you've probably guessed by now, that person is you. You are always there with yourself. So, you need to be your own cheerleader, the one loving yourself. You can do this by talking to yourself in a way that encourages your growth. You can do it both during times when you need encouragement and times when you have achieved success. By recognizing that you are constantly talking to yourself, you can make a conscious effort to talk to yourself in a supportive way. You can be the one who reminds yourself to do things, who encourages yourself when life's situations get tough, and who celebrates your minor and major successes. Remind yourself to perform the actions that will work out for your good rather than self-sabotage.

For example, you can give yourself kind permission to sleep if you are tired. This advice can come with a reminder to set the alarm that will wake you up to study at a later time when your mind and body are refreshed. This trumps trying to struggle through your exhaustion and beating yourself up. You can remind yourself to pack all the things that you need for the day ahead. You just need to treat yourself like somebody who loves you dearly—somebody who would go to the moon and back for you. That's how you have to talk to and treat yourself. This is the inner communication that promotes self-love.

So, let's discuss this idea of self-love a little bit more. What does it look like to love yourself, and what could be blocking you from doing all those little things that help you make the best decisions for yourself every day?

What Self-Love Looks Like

Kindness

What I learned was to always be kind to myself, no matter the circumstances. Treating myself with some loving kindness helped me make many great decisions, like not giving up an instrument because sight reading took me a little longer to grasp than my classmates. I would tell myself kind things like, "Practice makes perfect" and "I couldn't play this song three weeks ago, but now I can play it by heart!" This is a much better way to talk to yourself than breaking yourself down with negative self-talk.

Ask yourself what you can do to be kinder to yourself today, and then do it. Being kind to yourself means bringing comfort to your world, whether this is by avoiding the cold, keeping hunger at bay, or staying away from people who are unkind to you. Always choose the best option for yourself. What you tell yourself over and over will stick in your subconscious mind, so make sure it's positive!

Acceptance

You may not have some features you admire or possess the skills that others have in some areas. Most people can find a few things not to like about themselves, their lives, and their circumstances. However, if you were able to ask everyone you know in an honest conversation, you'd be surprised to find out the good attributes that you possess. Some of these are traits that other people wish they had, things that they see as missing from their lives. Yet, you might be living with the one thing that they wish they had and not even recognize it! So, the best thing to do is accept yourself. Accept the parts of you that you consider faulty, and embrace the parts of you that you consider fabulous. Who you are and what you have are the tools in your toolbox of life. So, instead of complaining about your tools and envying the tools that other people have, appreciate and enhance what you possess. Accepting all the parts of yourself can teach you how to turn some of your weaknesses and undervalued aspects into strengths. Almost every adult has something about themselves that they weren't originally crazy about, but it becomes their favorite part of themselves, whether it's a physical trait (like freckles or curly hair, etc.) or a part of their personality (being a book worm or super-sensible, etc.). Maybe later on in life, their curly hair landed them the cover of a fashion magazine, or maybe the bookworm ended up coding awesome video games for a massive company!

Patience

You might judge yourself for not doing things as fast as you expected to or as fast as other people might get things done. But if you recognize that you have your own pace and rhythm that aligns with who you are, you can stop judging and start celebrating—just be patient enough to learn the skills that others might appear to have mastered effortlessly. You can bet that it took them a really long time to master their skills behind the scenes! Remember, some of your favorite influencers spent countless hours building their followings, editing thumbnails and videos, etc, before they blew up. Success doesn't just happen overnight, even when it looks that way. Instead of comparing yourself to others, compare your current efforts against your previous efforts. If you are making your best attempts and stepping up as you aim higher in life, then you are making progress. It is really healthy to respect that about yourself.

For example, when I learned to play the guitar, it was difficult in the beginning. I could not master the placement of my fingers for playing each note. There were times when I used to cringe at my playing because each song I tried to play sounded like I was auditioning for a musical horror movie! Over time and with hours of practice, I found my musical skills improving enough to be invited to join a band. The hours of practice had required patience—patience enough to listen to my terrible music while believing that I would one day play this new instrument at a level where my band actually had fans.

So, practice patience through the difficult times when you are learning a new skill. You wouldn't even know of all the musicians, actors, and influencers you look up to if they just gave up and didn't practice patience. So keep going! Your abilities will greatly improve—sometimes to the point where you gain enough confidence to share your new skill with others. Recognize that the need to be patient with yourself applies to all areas of your life.

Value

Appreciate yourself. Value yourself. Develop a sense of self-worth. Know that you are valuable simply because you exist. Recognize that your life has a purpose, even if you have not yet discovered it. You must be proud of yourself and your past accomplishments. You must believe that you are going to accomplish so much in the future. You are valuable, and all your efforts are valuable.

Strengths

WHAT AM I AMAZING AT?

Qualities

WHAT MAKES ME, ME?

Uniqueness

WHAT MAKES ME SHINE?

Accomplishments

WHAT ARE YOU PROUD OF?

Recognizing When Self-Love Is Missing

Not Loving Yourself

In order to truly love others around you, you must discover how to truly love yourself first. This is one of life's most important truths!

Discouraging Yourself From Trying New Things

If you never step out of your norm, you might not discover all of the amazing things the world has to offer. That exotic dish that you just heard about? Well, that could be your new favorite food. And you never would have known if you hadn't had the courage to try it! The same goes for new sports, style, music, or even hanging out with somebody that you wouldn't think you would click with.

Telling Yourself You Are Not Good Enough

Don't be so hard on yourself! Instead, appreciate that you tried. Some people are so scared that they are not good enough that they never get around to trying what they really want to do. Even if you fail, you will have a new experience, and you will learn so much from it! Failure is a major part of success. Anyone successful has failed thousands of times, which is why they have learned what not to do. This is just as important as learning the correct steps!

Try to avoid calling yourself names like "stupid," "silly," or "slow" because then you are bullying yourself. And subconsciously, you are conditioning your brain to believe these things are true! You would never say these kinds of words to your best friend, so why would you do it to yourself? Whenever you have those moments of being mean to yourself, just turn the negative words into positive ones, and you will be amazed at how life mirrors this positivity back to you!

Believing That You Do Not Deserve Something

Believe that you deserve good things. If other people deserve goodness, so do you. There is no reason for you to deserve less. There is no one more important than you; no one is more important than anyone else. So whatever you want, go for it because you deserve it!

Dwelling on the Past

Every second of your life counts, so the time that you spend dwelling on the past or any negative experience is taking away from the now. Think about the countless hours you might spend thinking about the past that you cannot control. The time in fourth grade when you made your best friend cry or that time that you tripped in front of the whole class? I bet you barely even remembered these little moments a month or a year afterward, so instead of dwelling, look forward, not backward.

Turning Negative Self Talk to Positive Self Talk

Now that we recognize what self love is, when it's missing, and the tools to help you begin this self love journey, let's do an activity to rewire how we subconsciously and consciously talk to ourselves!

The first worksheet is filled out to give you some ideas on how to fill it out. Now is your time to reflect and fill in the blank version with your personal answers!!

TURN NEGATIVE SELF TALK TO POSITIVE SELF TALK

TURN THIS   TO THIS

TURN THIS	TO THIS
I don't know how to	I'll try my best & practice
I don't have time	I'll make the time
This is too hard	It might be challenging, but i've got this
I made a mistake	I learned a lesson that will help me grow

TURN NEGATIVE SELF TALK TO POSITIVE SELF TALK

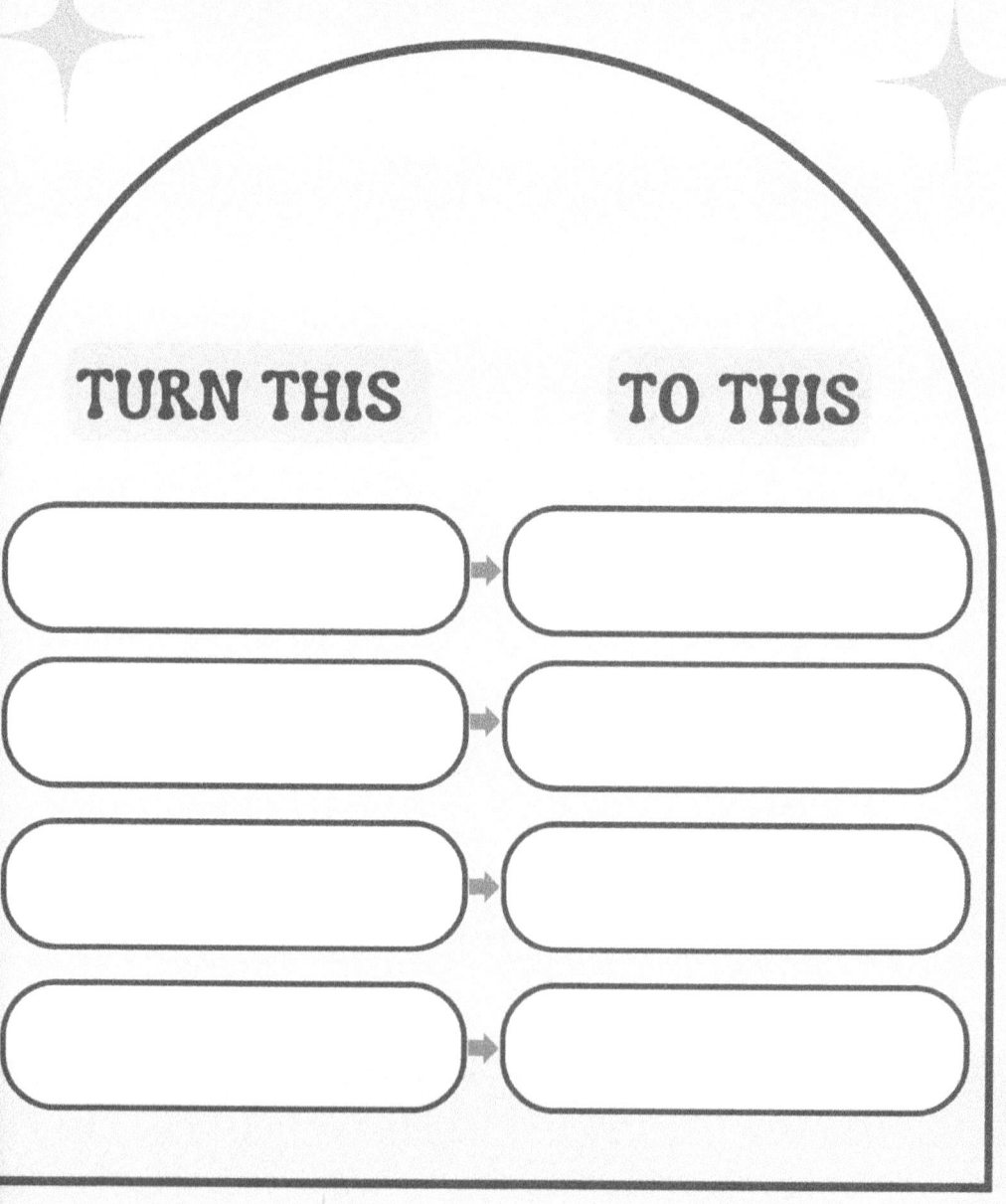

TURN THIS

TO THIS

CHAPTER TWO

Personal Development Life Skills

How To Crush Goals, Create Routines, Develop Powerful Habits, and Manage Time Like a Boss!

Now that you know all about self-love, it's time to start thinking about your dream life. To get there, we'll start with goal setting. It's fun to think about what you want to achieve in your life, but having a proper system will help you realistically achieve them! This is where the D.R.E.A.M system comes in.

D.R.E.A.M Goals

If you dream it, you can achieve it. In this case, D.R.E.A.M refers to the acronym I use for setting and reaching my goals. Start by writing your goals down in your notebook or journal. A great place to start is by knowing whether your goals are long-term goals or short-term goals. A long-term goal (think a few years or even longer) would be to become a famous singer, and a short-term goal (think 2 weeks to 6 months) would be to get an A on your math test next month. Short-term goals might take even a few hours to a few months and are very specific, whereas long-term goals might take several years to a lifetime and are a lot more ambitious. With long-term goals, there is lots of room for change along the journey.

To work through this section, start with a list of 10 items that you would like to accomplish within the next 12 months. Leave a few extra lines under each item on the list. This will give you space later to write out why you want to accomplish that particular goal. For now, let's look at the D.R.E.A.M acronym for setting goals. This will help you when writing your list and make it easier to accomplish the goals you have set out.

Define

To keep moving, you need a destination. Otherwise, you are driving your life when no GPS direction has been set for it. You might end up driving around in circles. Define where you want to go and what it looks like. Take time out to think about how long it will take to get there and how much effort you need to put in to get to your destination.

When you define your goals, it is best to imagine a future moment. Close your eyes and think about your future self at the moment when you have just achieved the goal you originally decided on. What does it look like, and what are you doing at that imagined moment? Who are you with? Where are you? How did you get there, and how do you feel now that you have accomplished this goal? Can you envision why you took the necessary actions to get there?

An effective method for doing this is to imagine the successful outcome of what you are aiming for. If you are planning on acing the math test, imagine the moment when you receive your test results. Where will you be? Who will be around you? Who will give you the news? How will you feel when you receive that news? If you close your eyes and imagine the moment down to how you will feel, then you are well on your way to dreaming an achievable dream. If you can envision this moment and then put it into words, you will have defined your goal in a way that makes it easier to accomplish!

Realistic

When you set out your list of goals, make sure that it is realistic for your situation. Any challenges to achieving your goal should have solutions that are within reach (at least for now). For example, if you want to be recognized as the best all-around student, you will need to excel in all your subjects. You may face challenges in some subjects that are harder for you than others. However, if you can get help with the difficult subjects, your goal could be accomplished within a period of 12 months. Therefore, this kind of goal is realistic. An unrealistic goal is one that may not be accomplished by you just yet, even when using the tools and resources you have within your reach. If achieving the goal takes a longer time than you have available to you, or the resources are not within reach, then the goal is not realistic. You can come back to this goal when you're more ready and the timing is right!

If the goal can be accomplished over a longer period, then a good idea is to review how much time you will need to achieve it. Some goals may need 4 years rather than 4 months to accomplish. An example of this kind of goal is "graduating high school with at least a 3.5 GPA." This goal requires you to be consistent with your mid-terms, homework, and your attendance before you can accomplish it. While it is an achievable goal in the long term, it's not considered a short-term goal because it usually takes about 4 years to graduate.

For now, focus on the goals that you can accomplish with the tools and resources you currently have. For goals that cannot be accomplished within a 12-month period, remember that your short-term goals are stepping stones toward them. When you have time, you can do the exercise to determine what is needed to accomplish long-term tasks realistically. This realistic thought process can also help you decide on the amount of time that you need. If something will take years to accomplish, try to map out the steps that will eventually get you there. With these long-term goals, go over them yearly to see if they still align with who you are now or if they need to be updated in some way. Remember, you're ever-changing, so your goals might grow with you as you grow!

Easy

Once you have defined your goal and made it realistic, let's see how we can break it down into small pieces so that it's easier to achieve! Breaking down your goal into these smaller steps will make it easier for you to manage. For example, finishing the year at the top of the class is a huge goal to aim for.

If you break it down into small steps, then it means that you will need to:

♥ Study for at least 40 to 60 minutes every night before a test and aim for at least a B grade or higher.

♥ Attend all your classes. (Did you know that studies show if you miss 10 days of school in a year, then you are 25% less likely to go to college?!)

♥ If you don't understand something your teacher said in class, put your hand up and ask additional questions. (Remember, there is NO SUCH THING as a stupid question when it comes to your education.) When you ask a question, you become what's known as an "active learner." This means that you are interacting with the information instead of just letting it go into one ear and out the other. Studies show that this type of active learning helps information stick in your mind much better!

♥ Do some extra research by reading books from the school library or looking online. You can even make it fun by studying with your friends! Remember, you are lucky enough to live in a time where information is everywhere. This means you can earn from podcasts, videos, games, books, and more!

From a single goal, you now have at least five different actions that can be performed for every test. All these tests put together will have an impact on your overall goal of becoming top in your class. While the bigger goal might seem difficult to reach at first glance, breaking down the goal into smaller goals makes it easier to tackle!

Action

Okay, to take action, it's good to stay organized! Create a schedule for each day. You'll want a daily, weekly, and monthly planner to stay on track. With your planner, you can do things like make a to-do list, habit-tracker, goal-tracker, etc.

When filling out your planner, it's good to prioritize what needs to be done by order of importance and focus on urgent tasks first. However, make sure that you make time later for the tasks that might not be as urgent. To make it fun you can even draw cute pictures and add stickers!

Sharing your plans with supportive friends and family will help you, as they can remind you and encourage you whenever you feel too tired to focus. These people will keep you accountable to your goals and can be your accountability partners as you move forward.

By doing the activities daily that chip away at your larger goals, you will start to build habits around them. Once the habits have become a part of you, you will start to perform these tasks without even looking at your schedule! Your daily habits will help you achieve those long-term goals by achieving mini milestones along the way.

Below is a version of a habit tracker. For example, if you want to study one hour per day, write that under healthy habit, and mark each day you complete the task. Of course, you can purchase a habit tracker planner, but even better, there are free options, such as finding a habit tracker template online and then printing it out or simply copying this example to a notebook or piece of paper!

Then, you can do the same for the daily planner. These are two great tools to help with the "action" portion of D.R.E.A.M goals!

Healthy Habit	M	T	W	TH	F	S	SUN

Daily Planner

TODAY'S TOP PRIORITIES

TO DO'S

FOR TOMORROW

DAILY SCHEDULE

7AM

8AM

9AM

10AM

11AM

12PM

1PM

2PM

3PM

4PM

5PM

6PM

7PM

Manifest

Imagine that life is one big mirror reflecting back to you the things that you believe deep down. Well, that's kind of how life works! Your favorite singers BELIEVE that they are really good at singing! And so, their world reflects that.

Now, let's use this reflection idea when it comes to your goals. If you truly believe that you will achieve your goals and get rid of any blocks to these beliefs (I will show you how to do this in a second), then life can only mirror your achievement back to you! This is known as manifestation. Sometimes, it can take a little time to manifest big goals, but smaller goals can manifest quite quickly. But it all comes down to what you BELIEVE!

Did you know that if a radio transmitter is giving out a specific frequency (let's say "frequency Z"), then a radio receiver (like a walkie-talkie, for example) that is tuned into the same "frequency Z" will pick up that radio transmission? This is the same way manifestation works! If you transmit a frequency (like a radio transmitter) with your thoughts of being super excited and in love with your goal, like a long-term goal of becoming a great actor, then the universe will match the frequency of your excitement with a manifestation in your life, such as acting auditions, parts in school plays, or even parts in movies or TV shows! This is because the potential of you being a great actor already exists in the universe as information that matches the frequency of your excitement about it.

You are simply attracting that information to you. On a scientific level, this is known as quantum entanglement. But lots of people also call it synchronicity. Everything in the universe is simply information vibrating at a specific frequency that you can match if you want to!

So how can we do this? One way is to practice saying positive affirmations, like "I have all the power in me to get straight As in every test!". If you say it with excitement while visualizing holding your test paper with your teacher's massive A+ on it, you will match the frequency of that potential and attract it to you. Just make sure to remember that if you want to manifest something, you have to put the work in as well, so study hard!

So, when it comes to all of your D.R.E.A.M goals, manifesting with positive affirmations and visualization is key!

Vision Board

A great way of manifesting is creating a vision board. You can do a physical or digital version. With a digital vision board, find photos online of the things you want to manifest. For example, if you want to travel more, find specific photos of places you want to visit. If you want to work on your sense of fashion, save photos of outfits you want to recreate and inspire your wardrobe.

When creating a physical vision board, let your creativity flow! You can use a poster board, cardboard, paper, or anything you can glue photos to. You can use things like magazine cutouts, printed images from online, stickers, drawings, glitter, etc., to create your manifesting masterpiece!

The most important key to a vision board is keeping it in a place you can see all the time. Whether it's a physical one hung up in your bedroom or a digital one you made and put as your computer background.

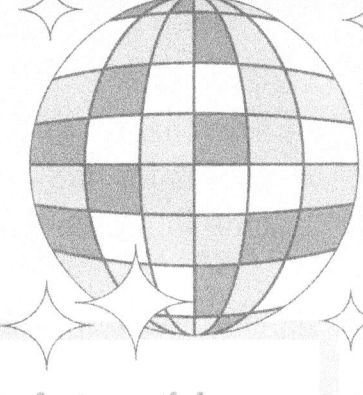

(Put photos, stickers, magazine clippings, & inspiring artwork here)

(Put photos, stickers, magazine clippings, & inspiring artwork here)

(Put photos, stickers, magazine clippings, & inspiring artwork here)

GOOD VIBES

(Put photos, stickers, magazine clippings, & inspiring artwork here)

TRUST YOUR VISION

(Put photos, stickers, magazine clippings, & inspiring artwork here)

Now that we know what each letter in D.R.E.A.M goals stands for and all of the wonderful tools to help us, it's time to curate your own specific goals.

The first worksheet is to reflect and write down ten of your goals and specific questions to ask yourself.

You will then pick one of those goals and break it down on the next worksheet with the dream goal system. The next page is an example to help you visualize how this works.

Just like the habit tracker, use the second worksheet as an example and write down the other nine goals on paper.

GOALS

10 GOALS I WANT TO ACHIVE THIS YEAR:

WHY ARE THESE GOALS SO IMPORTANT TO ME?

THINGS I CAN DO TO ACHIEVE THESE GOALS/THINGS
THAT MAY GET IN MY WAY:

D.R.E.A.M
GOALS

Define
WHAT EXACTLY DO YOU WANT TO ACHEIVE? WRITE DOWN YOUR SHORT TERM & LONG TERM GOALS.

Realistic
MAKE SURE TO SET REALISTIC EXPECTATIONS FOR YOURSELF. WRITE DOWN WHEN YOU ACTUALLY THINK THESE GOALS CAN BE ACHIEVED BY.

Easy
BREAK DOWN YOUR GOALS INTO TINY, EASY, & ACHIEVABLE STEPS.

Action
NOW IS THE TIME TO MAKE WORDS INTO ACTION! CREATE TO-DO LISTS, GOAL TRACKERS, & PLANNERS TO KEEP YOU ON TRACK!

Manifest
WRITE YOUR AFFIRMATIONS HERE & REPEAT THEM DAILY! SPEAK YOUR DREAM GOALS INTO EXISTENCE!

GOALS

EXAMPLE

Define	SHORT TERM GOAL EXAMPLE:
WHAT EXACTLY DO YOU WANT TO ACHEIVE? WRITE DOWN YOUR SHORT TERM & LONG TERM GOALS.	• GET AN "A" GRADE IN EVERY CLASS BY THE END OF THE FINAL SEMESTER.

Realistic	
MAKE SURE TO SET REALISTIC EXPECTATIONS FOR YOURSELF. WRITE DOWN WHEN YOU ACTUALLY THINK THESE GOALS CAN BE ACHIEVED BY.	• ON AVERAGE, A SEMESTER LASTS 15 WEEKS, SO THATS ALMOST 4 MONTHS TO ACHIEVE MY GOAL (WRITE DOWN THE SPECIFIC DATE). • THIS IS POSSIBLE BECAUSE I HAVE AN OLDER SIBLING WHO ACCOMPLISHED THIS LAST YEAR. 4 MONTHS IS PLENTY OF TIME TO ACHIEVE MY GOAL, & I BELIEVE IN MYSELF.

Easy	
BREAK DOWN YOUR GOALS INTO TINY, EASY, & ACHIEVABLE STEPS.	• I HAVE 6 CLASSES WHICH MEANS 6 A'S. • IF EACH CLASS GIVES ME HOMEWORK, I WILL TRACK HOW LONG EACH ASSIGNMENT TAKES & SET THAT TIME FOR MYSELF EACH NIGHT. (EXAMPLE: 15 MINS EACH CLASS = 90 MINS TOTAL) • EACH 90 MIN WINDOW I WORK EACH NIGHT, I WILL ELIMINATE DISTRACTIONS (TV, PHONE, LOUD PLACES). • I WILL TAKE ON ANY EXTRA CREDIT TO INCREASE MY CHANCES OF AN A. • I WILL COMMIT TO STUDYING ON THE WEEKEND.

Action	
NOW IS THE TIME TO MAKE WORDS INTO ACTION! CREATE TO-DO LISTS, GOAL TRACKERS, & PLANNERS TO KEEP YOU ON TRACK!	• CREATE A FOLDER FOR EACH CLASS. • EACH FOLDER WILL HAVE A TO-DO LIST FOR THE CLASS, AS WELL AS A HOMEWORK TRACKER, SO I DON'T MISS ANY ASSIGNMENTS. • I WILL KEEP A PLANNER SO I CAN BALANCE SCHOOL & MY PERSONAL LIFE. • I'LL USE BOOKS, APPS, & STUDY GROUPS TO HELP PREPARE FOR THE EXAMS. • I'LL TELL FAMILY, FRIENDS, OR A TEACHER MY GOALS SO THEY CAN HELP KEEP ME ACCOUNTABLE.

Manifest	
WRITE YOUR AFFIRMATIONS HERE & REPEAT THEM DAILY! SPEAK YOUR DREAM GOALS INTO EXISTENCE!	• WRITE DOWN AFFIRMATIONS (I AM CAPABLE OF MAKING STRAIGHT A'S, I CAN'T WAIT TO SEE ALL OF THE A'S ON MY FINAL REPORT CARD, ETC.) • I WILL PUT PHYSICAL COPIES OF MY AFFIRMATIONS NEAR MY MIRROR & FOLDER SO I CAN SEE THEM EASILY THROUGHOUT MY DAY. • I WILL AVOID USING NEGATIVE SELF-TALK SUCH AS, "I CAN'T," "I'LL NEVER GET THIS," ETC. • I WILL STAY POSITIVE, EVEN IF NEGATIVE THINGS COME MY WAY.

Positive Affirmations

When creating the statements for your affirmations, be careful with the words you use. Avoid wording that is negative or can cause you to doubt yourself. For example, avoid making statements such as "I hope to get accepted into drama club," as this sends a message to your subconscious mind that you are not sure. The purpose of creating affirmations is to send a message to your subconscious mind of the world you want to live in. The subconscious mind accepts positive, definitive statements. That is why a statement like "I will not fail my test" may backfire. The action words in that sentence are "fail my test." The words "I will not" are not positive and, therefore, cannot be acted upon. As a result, these words are discarded, and the mind focuses on the action words. That is why wording your statements positively is important. It is better to use statements like "I will join the drama club this year" and "I will receive a perfect test score." These types of positively worded statements are more effective for helping you manifest your goals.

Be selective about who you share your dreams with. Talk to those people who believe in your dreams and want you to accomplish them. Share your goals with them so they can visualize alongside you. In this way, you can speak your dreams into existence. Do not share your dreams with people who like to throw shade. Such people often do not believe in themselves or in other people's ability to achieve their goals. They will most likely discourage you and limit your beliefs. When you are manifesting, you will need to stay away from limiting beliefs, both within yourself and within others.

In the DREAM section, I asked you to imagine the moment when you have achieved your goal. When you are repeating your affirmations to yourself, it will help to remember that imagined moment. In this way, not only are you saying that you will receive a perfect test score, but you are also seeing and feeling what that reality will look like. When you do this, you get your mind ready to live that reality, so when the day finally arrives, it will feel like you have been through the experience before. You will have mentally lived through the experience so many times that your reality will finally collide with what has been in your head for some time.

As you successfully complete each daily task, write it down in your journal. Over time, you will find that accomplished tasks bring results. Write these down as well. Doing this will encourage you to keep on moving toward your goal. Reviewing it from time to time will also confirm to you that the small daily steps you are taking are worthwhile and effective.

Here are some examples of positive affirmations. Now use the blank version to create your own!

Positive Affirmations

I am...
beautiful inside & out.

I am...
capable of anything.

I am...
my own version of perfect.

I am...
more than enough.

I am...
stronger with each day that passes by.

I am...
confident from the inside out.

Positive Affirmations

I am...

I am...

I am...

I am...

I am...

I am...

CHAPTER THREE

Social & Relationship Life Skills

**How to Be THAT Girl,
Face Any Social Setting, & Illuminate Every Room You Walk Into!**

Are you someone who feels comfortable around family but gets social anxiety around people you don't know? You might even stumble over your words when somebody asks a question or hope that you can disappear down a rabbit hole.

In this chapter, we'll discuss how to navigate the wonderful world of people. You will discover how to overcome the heart-pounding feelings of social anxiety and be able talk to people with confidence.

How to Carry Yourself With These Manner Life Hacks!

Good manners leave people with a good impression of who you are. This can result in you being welcome into different social situations. People will enjoy being around you and look forward to meeting with you again.

This will not always be because you wowed them with hilarious stories or told them about your interesting past. It will be because they will feel comfortable in your presence. Manners aren't just about pleases and thank you's; they are about how you carry yourself and so much more. I am about to share some social life hacks with you!

At the Table

So many social engagements take place around mealtimes. This makes it important for you to know how to carry yourself around this type of social setting, whether it happens in somebody's home or at a restaurant.

♥ When a meal is served at somebody's house, the host will often appreciate it if you offer to help set the table. After the meal is finished, you can also offer to help clear the table. Stacking the dishwasher or helping to wash the dishes may also be welcomed.

♥ Try to keep an eye on your posture and body language and engage with those around you during the meal. Body language includes keeping your elbows off the dinner table and keeping your mouth closed while you finish chewing your food. Don't be that girl who chews with her mouth open! It sounds like a no-brainer, but sometimes it's easy to forget.

♥ Try to engage in polite conversation and keep your hands away from your cell phone if you have one. Rule of thumb: you don't want to seem rude by being on your phone the whole time, so be mindful and think about putting it away!

♥ When getting up from the table, it is good to excuse yourself first. Just a small "Excuse me," said out loud goes a long way. Then, you can stand up and step aside for a visit to the restroom or wherever you need to go.

♥ Remember not to use your fork in your right hand as though it were a spoon. Instead, try to keep your fork in your left hand and your knife in your right hand. If you want to put them down when you are talking, you can rest the tips of the cutlery against the edge of your plate.

♥ When you have finished eating, place your fork and knife together in the middle of your plate.

♥ If the table has more than one set of cutlery laid out for more than a single course, remember to use the cutlery that's on the outside first and work your way toward the plate with each course.

Meeting New People

Knowing how to engage with new people is a useful skill to have. Greet new people with a smile while maintaining eye contact. Looking into their eyes as you talk to them confirms that you care about their presence and respect them (everyone likes to be respected!). It also creates a connection between you. Smiling is contagious; a smile directed at someone you just met can totally turn their whole day around! If they are feeling anxious or unsure about the environment, it will let them know that you want to engage with them. In this way, a person who is looking around for somebody to talk to will sense your friendly energy.

Making Conversation

♥ Introduce yourself by giving your name and, if you feel comfortable, feel free to offer them a handshake. If you don't like shaking hands, you can smile at the person and give them a head nod, or even giving them a kind hand-waving gesture is enough. I even like to do a peace sign sometimes!

♥ Then, give the other person an opportunity to introduce themselves or ask them what their name is. You can then ask them a question about themselves that relates to the surroundings that you're in. For example, if you are at a music show, it can be as simple as asking them if they enjoyed the band. Even just giving them a compliment is an amazing way to start a conversation and make those around you feel comfortable!

♥ As you engage in conversation, show respect by listening as they express themselves. Wait until they finish their sentences before responding, and try not to interrupt them while they are talking. Instead, you can show that you are listening by smiling and nodding your head.

♥ Don't be the girl that gossips. Gossip can truly hurt and affect people differently. You never know what someone's going through at home or in their personal lives. I know it can be hard when you're engaged in conversation with friends to not talk about other people sometimes, but just try to be weary of speaking negatively about anyone. Try to be the one to steer the conversation in a positive direction when you speak about others.

♥ Give the person in front of you attention that will make them feel as though you value their presence. If you need to do something else, excuse yourself first before leaving the conversation.

Changes in Friendships

When you meet someone who has so much in common with you, this is someone who's definitely worth building a good friendship with! However, you spend years in middle school developing these friendships, but as you start to grow, some of your interests might change. You might discover new music, sports, or a new style that you really like, but maybe your current friends don't like this new kind of music. Or maybe you're starting to become more of a social butterfly, but some of your friends are still more on the shy side. It's okay to meet and become friends with new people. I know sometimes it feels like you're growing apart from your friends, but life is about growing and changing. Even though it may hurt to feel as though you are losing your friend, know that it will be okay over time. Change is a normal part of life, and the most important thing is to understand this so you can cope.

Know that friendships evolve and life changes.

Sometimes, friends even move to a new town. Try to accept and welcome changes as opportunities to learn new things that can open you up to new interests and opportunities. If you can make friends who share similar interests to yours, you will feel the growing distance between yourself and your old friend less intensely. Appreciate the good memories of things you have done together and maintain occasional contact with them if possible. However, keep evolving your life by making more friends who have interests similar to yours. That's how you can glow up in your relationships.

Boundary-setting mastery and how to send peer pressure packing!

Body Language

Body language is the way we send messages to other people without saying a word. Some examples of body language include smiling, frowning, head shaking, crossing arms, nodding, tilting the head, and crossing or uncrossing legs. All of the things I have just mentioned mean something different. If you understand how to read and interpret body language, you will know that some of the body language I just described sends a negative message, while other actions convey a positive message.

It is important to understand how to interpret body language. It helps improve the way you communicate with others. It can also alert you to potential danger in a situation. For example, if your friend's shoulders suddenly stiffen and they start frowning when they are talking to somebody, then this behavior might alert you to the fact that they are no longer feeling comfortable with the current conversation. If this happens, it may be good to swoop in and find out if your friend needs a diversion so that they can leave an uncomfortable conversation or place and feel safe.

Here are some tell-tale body language signals that you can recognize in social situations:

Positive body language signs (someone is comfortable):

♥ Arms open

♥ Standing up straight

♥ Eye contact

♥ Smiling

♥ Leaning in when listening to someone

♥ Arms hanging at sides of body comfortably

Negative body language signs (someone is uncomfortable):

♥ Arms crossed

♥ Slouching

♥ Avoiding eye contact (eyes looking down, nervously scanning the room)

♥ Nail biting

♥ Fidgeting

♥ Rapid blinking

Intuition

Have you ever felt your "spidey senses" tingling or heard that phrase before? This is a part of your intuition that keeps you safe. For example, maybe you had a gut feeling that you should stay home instead of going to that party, and the next day, you find out that everyone caught a stomach bug. On the other hand, do you ever get that feeling in your gut that you just knew you had to do something or go somewhere? Like the urge to go to your favorite clothing store, and when you get there, you see that there is a huge 60% sale off of everything and those boots you wanted? Well, they only had one pair left, and they happened to be in your size! See how intuition works to both keep you safe and lead you to amazing luck so long as you listen to it!?

Picking up on body language is also a type of intuition. Our bodies automatically communicate via body language to ourselves and others, whether we want them to or not. You can notice this if you pay attention to expressions and body movements next time you talk to somebody. See if their body signals align with what they are saying. If a person's body is giving off a different message than the one coming out of their mouth, it would be wise to be cautious with how you engage with them. Do not immediately trust their words, as their body might be telling you that they are lying. It is also extremely helpful to observe your own body language to understand the signals your body may be giving you about a situation!

Sometimes, your body will give off signals to show discomfort in a situation before you have consciously become aware of something being wrong. In these cases, your body will feel uneasy even though you are not sure why. You won't know how to explain what it is, except that you seem to be getting certain vibes that make you uneasy. If your body is giving your mind signals that it is not comfortable, it is your intuition.

Your intuition acts as an early warning system to warn you of imminent danger. In these situations, ask yourself why your intuition is sending you "vibes." Understand your physical and mental boundaries and stop any conversation where these are not respected or where you feel uncomfortable. This means that your mental boundaries have been crossed. Don't be afraid to excuse yourself from a situation that makes you feel uncomfortable. An uncomfortable situation could potentially turn into a threatening one. You shouldn't have to be in situations where you don't feel safe, comfortable, and happy. Always look out for yourself, and don't try to please others if you're not comfortable!

Maintaining Physical Boundaries

Maintaining physical boundaries helps you to maintain your joy. People who want to stand too close or put their arms around you when they are not your close friends are crossing physical boundaries. Speak up if you feel uncomfortable with something that somebody is doing because you feel they are invading your space. Let them know that they are crossing a physical boundary and that you are not comfortable with it. Don't be afraid to stand your ground (this is not the time to worry about what people think!). Ask them to stop and change their behavior. If they are a decent person, they will respect you enough to continue the conversation from a comfortable distance. If they do not alter their behavior, let them know that you're not comfortable and remove yourself from the situation.

Maintaining physical boundaries is not only about protecting your personal space. It is also about knowing what you will not allow yourself to do. Once you have decided on your boundaries, do not allow people to try and force you to change your mind. As a pre-teen, you will often face situations like this. Your teenage years may present you with some tough choices to make. However, if someone is pressuring you to do anything that doesn't align with your values or boundaries, you can respectfully decline, and the funny thing is, saying no and staying true to who you really are by not giving into other people's wants actually gets you a ton more respect! You do not even need to give a reason to anybody for rejecting certain ideas and activities. You do not owe them anything, and fulfilling what they want is not your responsibility. Those around you need to respect the fact that you have made a personal choice. If they press you for a reason, explain to them that it is your personal decision, your life, your body, your personal space.

At the end of the day, no one should ever make you feel like you should:

♥ Change yourself

♥ Lie for someone else

♥ Be mean to someone else

♥ Accept any physical touch

♥ Take any substances

♥ Partake in any bad behavior

Not one of these things is cool, even if someone tries to make you think they are. Do you know what's cool? Having self-respect, self-love, and standing strong in your boundaries! Some of these things listed above could potentially change the course of your life, so don't give anyone but yourself that power.

Types of

Boundaries

Physical
- Privacy
- Personal boundaries
- Personal space

Material
- How you treat your personal property
- How you allow others to respect, use, & treat your physical possessions

Time
- How youre willing to spend your time
- Respecting your time enough to decline

Emotional
- Respecting & protecting your feelings
- What you're willing to share emotionally

Verbal
- What you feel comfortable talking about
- What you don't feel comfortable talking about
- How you allow someone to speak you

Personal
- Allowing yourself the freedom to have your own thoughts, opinions, values, & beliefs

Bullies

Bullies are people who deliberately cross mental and physical boundaries. Bullies may try to force you into doing something that you do not want to do. They could even do something offensive in an attempt to get a physical or emotional reaction from you. This is how they cross physical boundaries.

They may also use hurtful words in an attempt to draw a response out of you. They will throw shade just to see what you will do. In these cases, they are trying to manipulate your thinking and are crossing mental boundaries. They may try to break down your self-confidence by calling you names or encouraging others to engage with you negatively.

You must recognize that bullies are insecure, extremely scared, and hurt people who are suffering deep down. No one who is truly happy and secure inside treats others badly on purpose. Their actions are an attempt to build up their confidence by destroying yours. In this way, they attempt to turn your positive energy into negative energy. Engaging with them by trying to bully them back, either physically or with words, is not a good idea. It merely draws you into the trap of negativity where they are most comfortable, and you're better than that.

Instead, do your best to draw boundaries between yourself and the bullies and steer clear of them. Maintain your inner confidence. The less of a reaction you show by embodying your powerful self-respect and boundaries that we just talked about, the more they will realize that they are powerless to affect you and will eventually give up. A good rule of thumb is to keep really good friends around you while you're feeling uncomfortable because there is power in numbers, and never be afraid to confide in a trusted adult. Bullies might make you feel like if you tell an adult, then the bullying will get worse. However, this is often not the case (they are just trying to control the situation out of fear of getting in trouble), and adults usually have a lot of ways to end bullying.

Cyberbullying

If bullying occurs in an online situation, do your best to not engage. Instead, report their posts or comments to the owners of the platform. Take screenshots or print out the offensive communication immediately so you have evidence. Block the bully from engaging with your profile. Cyberbullying doesn't just happen on social media; it also happens through online gaming, text messages, emails, etc. When dealing with cyberbullying, the same boundaries we discussed earlier apply; only in these cases, you have the magical power of the block and report buttons! Did you know that in most states, there are laws in place for regular bullying and cyberbullying where schools help step in? So just know that there is so much out there to help you. Don't stoop to their level and send mean comments back or post anything mean because sometimes what goes up on the internet might have long-lasting effects.

What Boundaries Sound Like

NO.

I'M NOT COMFORTABLE WITH
THIS TOPIC,
SO I AM GOING TO
REMOVE MYSELF
FROM THE CONVERSATION.

I NEED A
MOMENT.

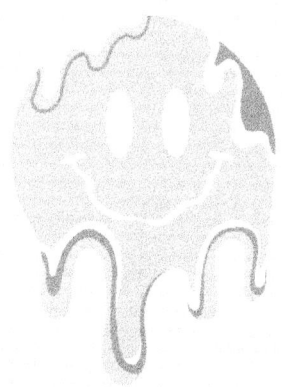

I RESPECT YOUR OPINION
AND FEELINGS, BUT I GIVE
MYSELF PERMISSION TO
HAVE MINE AS WELL.

I AM DOING WHAT'S
BEST FOR ME.

I DON'T NEED TO
EXPLAIN WHY
THIS MAKES ME FEEL
UNCOMFORTABLE.

CHAPTER FOUR

Practical Life Skills

Ways to be Uniquely Independent At Home & Beyond!

Reading Military Time

The military 24-hour clock differs from the 12-hour version we're used to. In the military, it helps avoid confusion between instructions that need to be carried out during the daytime and those intended for nighttime. Military time is important to understand because it's not only used in the army; you may see it used throughout your daily life! It's handy to know in emergency situations, and it's used across many time zones, countries, and industries.

The morning hours are the same for both military time and civilian time (civilian time means the regular 12-hour clock that we're familiar with). After midday, however, instead of reverting to 1 p.m., the military clock adds the 1 to the 12. For them, 1 o'clock in the afternoon is 13:00, or 13 hundred hours.

This means that when you are reading military time, you will need to reverse the steps for any time after midday. Simply subtract 12 from the time on the 24-hour military clock. An even easier way to do this is to subtract 2 and ignore the first digit. In this way, 18 hundred hours is read as 6 o'clock in the evening.

Military Time

Standard Time	Military Time	Standard Time	Military Time
12:00 AM	00:00/ 24:00	12:00 PM	12:00
1:00 AM	01:00	1:00 PM	13:00
2:00 AM	02:00	2:00 PM	14:00
3:00 AM	03:00	3:00 PM	15:00
4:00 AM	04:00	4:00 PM	16:00
5:00 AM	05:00	5:00 PM	17:00
6:00 AM	06:00	6:00 PM	18:00
7:00 AM	07:00	7:00 PM	19:00
8:00 AM	08:00	8:00 PM	20:00
9:00 AM	09:00	9:00 PM	21:00
10:00 AM	10:00	10:00 PM	22:00
11:00 AM	11:00	11:00 PM	23:00

Using a Fire Extinguisher

It's better to learn about using a fire extinguisher now than to be flustered in the event that you need one.

The PASS Method

The PASS method is the easiest method to remember when you are in an emergency. Memorizing these steps will help you stay levelheaded and act fast before the blaze spreads.

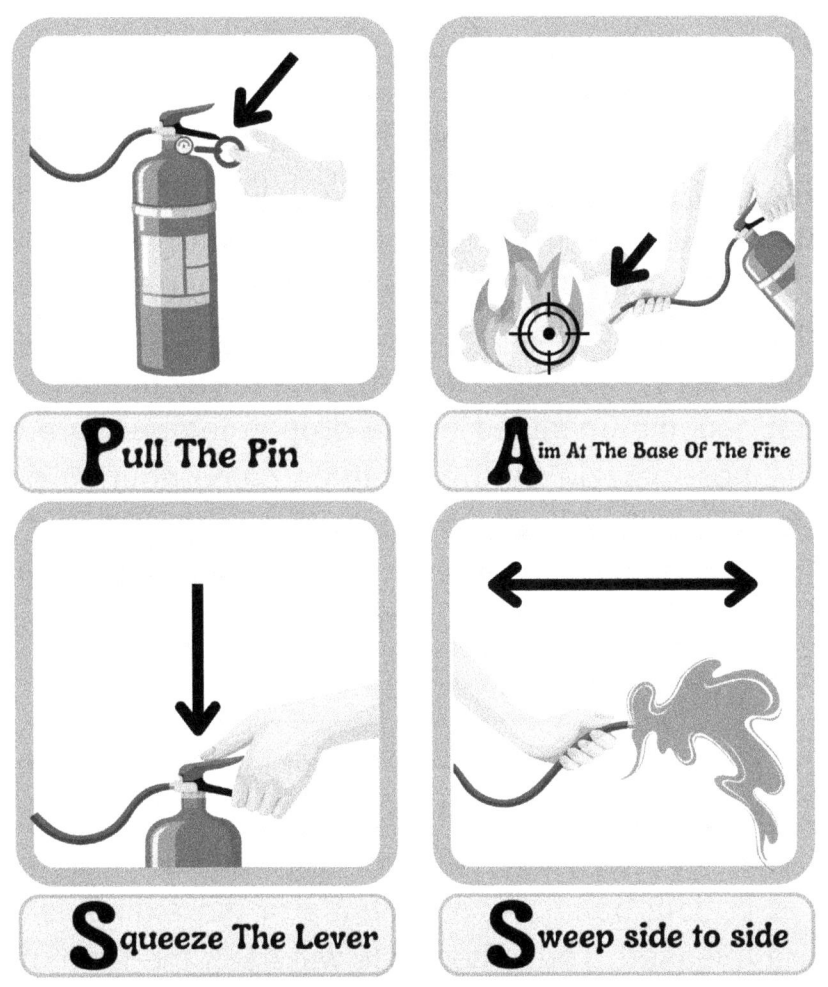

Pull The Pin

Aim At The Base Of The Fire

Squeeze The Lever

Sweep side to side

1. Pull out the safety pin from the top of the fire extinguisher. This safety pin holds the handle in place. It also serves to keep the contents safely inside the extinguisher so they do not spill out unnecessarily. When you pull it out, make sure you are standing at a safe distance of about eight feet away from the fire. Stand with your back to the nearest exit so you have an escape route should the flames prove too challenging to put out.

2. Aim the fire extinguisher hose toward the base of the fire. Once you have pulled the pin, hold the extinguisher so the hose is facing the fire rather than you. The point at which you hold the hose should not be too close to the point from which the contents come out. Rather, hold it so that you can easily direct it yet not become impacted by the drop in temperature on the hose nozzle as the contents come pouring out. Your other hand can hold onto the bottom handle of the extinguisher. This is below the handle you pulled the pin from. You can grip this bottom handle as you set up your aim.

3. Squeeze down on the lever to release the contents. This means holding both handles together. The top handle acts as a lever. When it is brought down toward the bottom handle, the contents of the extinguisher are released. These contents will be in the form of a white foam or a white powder.

4. Sweep over the fire by moving the hose from side to

side over the base of the flames. You can gradually move closer to the fire as it reduces in intensity. Continue to use the extinguisher until all the flames and any flickering embers have been fully put out. If the fire seems to get out of hand, it is better to use the exit that is at your back so you are safely out of harm's way. Somebody should have already phoned the fire department, and they will be on the way to deal with the growing flames.

5. Once you have used the fire extinguisher, ensure that it is replaced or refilled as soon as possible. This will ensure that it is ready for the next fire emergency that arises.

Hanging a Picture

Making your living space comfortable to relax in involves adding your personal touch to it. One of the best ways to do this is to add pictures. This could be in the form of posters, paintings, or photographs. You can also hang other decorative items on the wall, like pinboards and plastic decor. The methods for putting these up are similar to that of hanging posters and paintings.

When putting up your pictures, it's good to be aware of what is and is not allowed on the walls. For example, if you are living in a rented house, you will find that the guidelines for hanging pictures are slightly different than if your parents or guardians own the home. Your parents are likely to be more lenient with how you put up pictures than the landlord of a rental unit.

If you are in a rental unit, it is better to use rental-friendly methods such as Blu Tack, hooks, and Command strips to hang pictures on the walls. In a home your parents or guardians own, you can use more owner-friendly and permanent methods, such as nails and screwdrivers. Whatever the living situation, always get approval from your parents or guardians regarding the method you are going to use.

Painter's Tape Hack for Hanging Pictures

This hack can be used to avoid playing guessing games when putting in nails for your pictures. It helps you get the location right the first time. The hack involves painter's tape to make sure that the holes for the nails are at the right distance from each other on the wall.

1. First, take the painter's tape and stick it along the back of the picture that you want to hang up. Make sure it goes over the holes the nails need to go through when you hang the picture on the wall. Use a pencil to make marks on the painter's tape. These marks should be in line with the hooks or holes that go over the nails when the painting is hung.

2. Now, take the tape off the back of the picture and put it on the wall. Use a spirit level to help you stick the tape onto the wall in a straight line.

3. Hammer the nails into the wall at the points marked by the pencil. This should be in alignment with the holes on the back of the picture.

4. Once the nails are in the wall, with just enough sticking out for you to hang your painting, remove the painter's tape. You can now hang your picture up. It will be perfectly straight, and the holes will be in the right places for hanging.

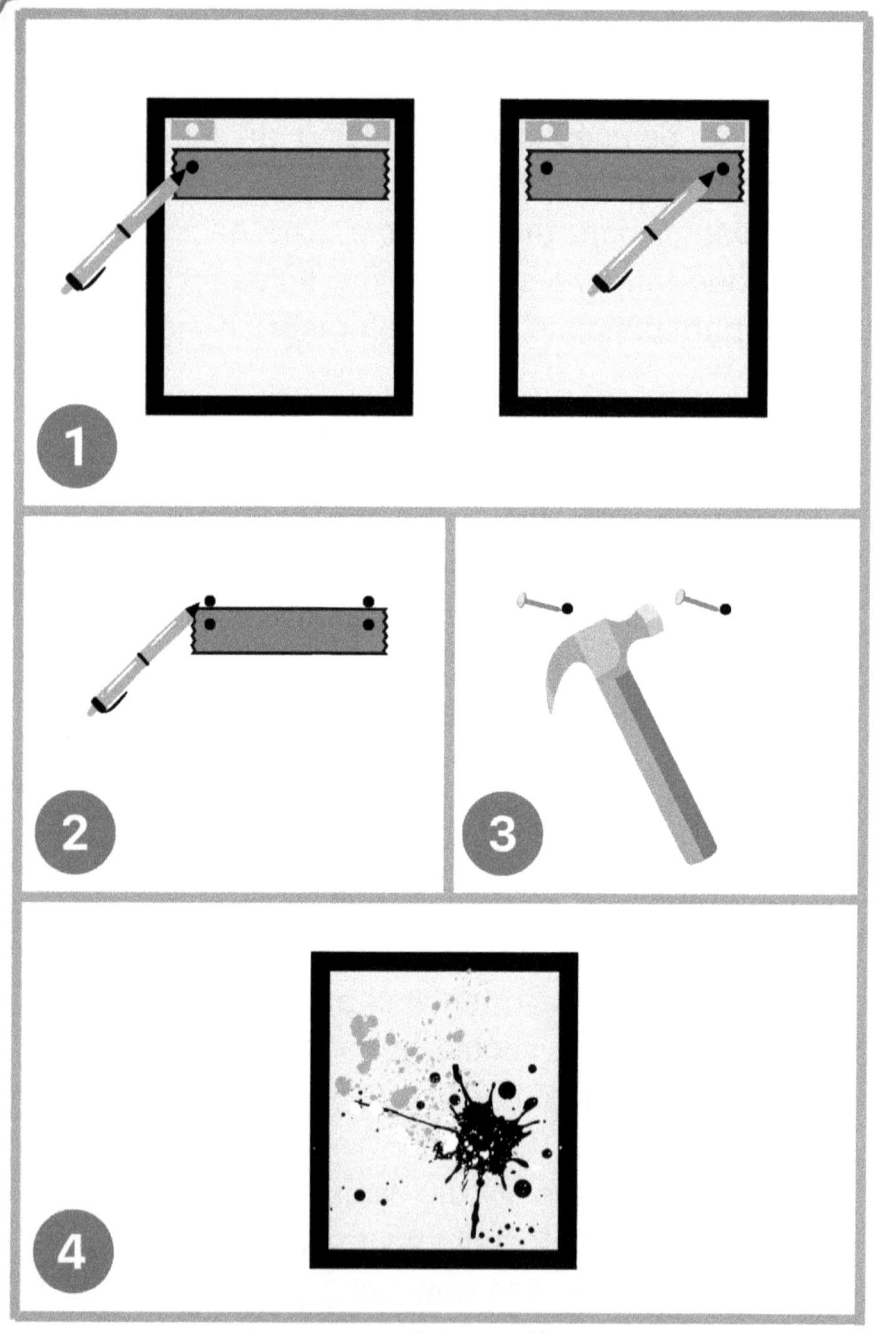

Using Command Strips

Command strips are double-sided sticky tape that provides a way to safely hang pictures on the wall. With them, you can do this in a way that causes less damage than nails and screws. It is not suitable for lightweight posters, as they can cause damage to the posters when removed. However, for framed pictures, they're easy to use. When you use them, avoid placing the pictures above beds and furniture where a weakened strip may result in the picture falling on top of someone.

♥ To use Command strips, start by cleaning the wall where the picture will hang. Use rubbing alcohol for this, as it removes any residue and makes the area more adhesive.

♥ Use the rubbing alcohol to clean the back of the picture frame as well.

♥ Remove any hooks or other hanging implements on the back of the frame so they don't interfere with the flat surface that makes the Command strips effective.

♥ Next, peel off the liner on one side of the Command strip and stick it firmly against the frame.

♥ Ensure that you have placed the Command strip on all sides of the frame to create an even weight distribution.

♥ Now, remove the liner on the opposite side of the Command strip and press the painting firmly against the wall. Press on each side to confirm that the Command strip is bonded to the wall.

♥ Should the day come when you need to remove the framed painting, grab the bottom corners and gently lift the painting away from the wall. The motion should result in the painting being peeled off from the wall. If there is some Command strip that stays on the wall rather than on the painting, gently peel it away.

Hanging Light Posters

For light posters that will be on your walls less permanently, you can use Blu Tack.

♥ To use this putty-like material to hang your posters, start by pinching a fingertip-sized piece off the strip.

♥ Next, you can roll this between your thumb and forefinger to create a small ball.

♥ Stick one small ball of Blu Tack to the back of each corner of the poster.

♥ Then, put the poster up on the wall.

♥ Press each corner firmly against the wall to ensure that the Blu Tack sticks the poster to the wall.

Blu Tack can be used for sticking other small items to the wall. Examples include ribbons, small crystals, fairy lights, and other small decorative items. Its benefit is that it's a non-permanent way to hang up decorations.

Doing Laundry

Reading the Care Label

Before starting, take time to familiarize yourself with the wash care labels on your clothes. This will help you look after them in the best possible way. The label will let you know what material each clothing item is made of. This can be cotton, wool, polyester, spandex, or a blend. Alongside this, it will tell you the best temperature for washing the item. The sign for this looks like a bowl filled with water that has the temperature number written on it. The circle on the label indicates whether the item can be dried in the drier. If the circle is crossed out, then you should not use the drier but, rather, air dry the clothing on the washing line, clothes hanger, or somewhere flat. The label also gives instructions on ironing. Using the iron icon, it tells you if the clothing should be ironed or not and at what temperature. Ironing at a higher temperature could lead to you burning a small hole in your clothes. So, if you are going to iron, make sure you set the iron to the right temperature before you mistakenly diminish your wardrobe.

LAUNDRY SYMBOLS

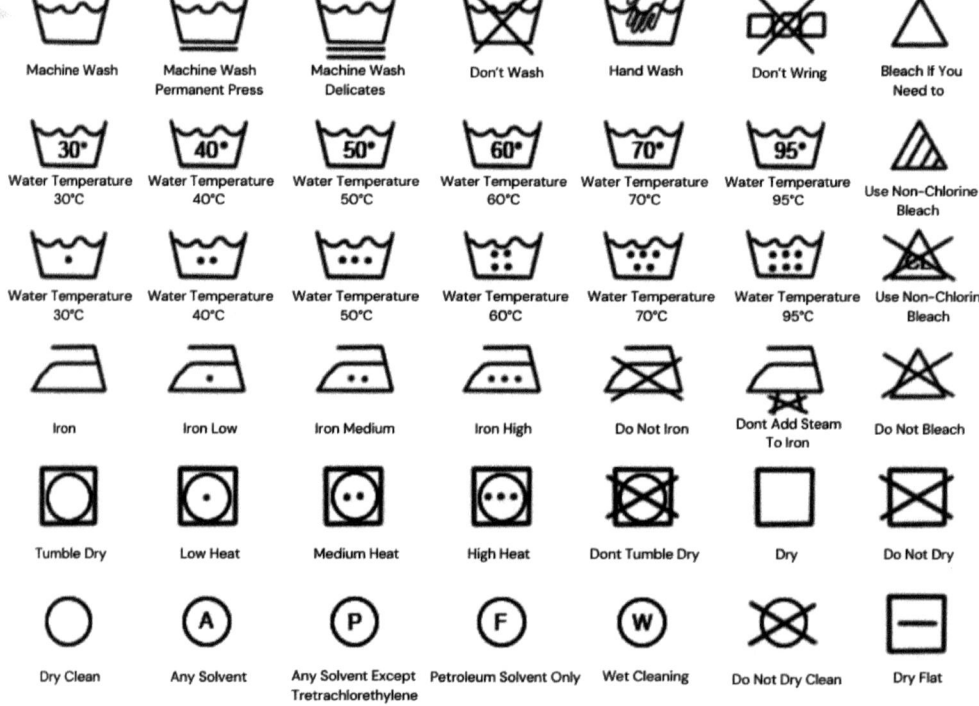

Machine Wash	Machine Wash Permanent Press	Machine Wash Delicates
Don't Wash	Hand Wash	Don't Wring
Bleach If You Need to		

Water Temperature 30°C	Water Temperature 40°C	Water Temperature 50°C
Water Temperature 60°C	Water Temperature 70°C	Water Temperature 95°C
Use Non-Chlorine Bleach		

Water Temperature 30°C	Water Temperature 40°C	Water Temperature 50°C
Water Temperature 60°C	Water Temperature 70°C	Water Temperature 95°C
Use Non-Chlorine Bleach		

Iron	Iron Low	Iron Medium
Iron High	Do Not Iron	Dont Add Steam To Iron
Do Not Bleach		

Tumble Dry	Low Heat	Medium Heat
High Heat	Dont Tumble Dry	Dry
Do Not Dry		

Dry Clean	Any Solvent	Any Solvent Except Tretrachlorethylene
Petroleum Solvent Only	Wet Cleaning	Do Not Dry Clean
Dry Flat		

Sorting

Before you put your clothes in the washing machine, sorting them into light and dark colors can help prevent a color catastrophe! The light colors will mostly consist of the white clothing items, as well as any well-worn and pale-colored clothes. The reason why this is done is to prevent your white clothes from becoming stained by dark items that can sometimes leak dye into the water during washing. These clothes can pose the danger of the color running and staining your white clothes. You might want to avoid the mistake I made of turning my pure whites into a pink-colored fashion disaster with the addition of a single dark-red T-shirt! That was so cringe-worthy! Just remember to always sort your items thoroughly before you start your laundry cycle!

Washing

Once you have sorted your clothes, it is often better to start washing the light-colored items first. Measure the detergent and fabric softener into their container. This is usually found near the top of the washing machine inside a little tray that pulls out. If you have a top loader washing machine, put the detergent into the machine before you put the clothes inside. The water will come into the machine from the bottom and dissolve any powdered soap before it is mixed in with the clothes. For front-loading machines, the water enters the washer after first mixing in with the detergent in the top tray.

Select the correct wash cycle. You will see options for both temperature and time. The short cycle is about 30 minutes and gets your clothes clean when there is no heavy-duty removal of stains needed. For this cycle, it is fine to put the temperature at lukewarm. Avoid using hot water, as this is best used on linen. Otherwise, it has the potential to cause clothes to shrink if the wash care labels are not read properly. Cold water washing is also effective for avoiding shrinkage or stretching and is appropriate to use when you are washing sweaters.

With the right temperature and time selected, you can press "start" to switch on the washing machine. If it is a top-loading washing machine, remember to add the fabric softener after about 20 minutes. It is best to mix this into some water first and not add it directly to the clothes. In this way, you will avoid staining your clothes with a stain from the fabric softener.

Drying

You can air dry clothes by hanging them on the washing line, or you can dry them in the tumble dryer. Clothes that have a "do not tumble dry" sign on the wash care label should not be placed in the dryer. This sign looks like a circle with a square around it. There is a big X on top of the sign. Clothes with this sign on them need to be air-dried.

For those clothes that can be placed in the dryer, look at the care label to help you select the right temperature. Some items can shrink if the temperature is too high. Place clothes that have a similar texture in the dryer at the same time. If clothes have different weight to each other, they can dry at different paces. For example, a sweater and a light shirt will dry at different times. To help speed up the drying process, you can put a clean, dry towel in the dryer. This will help to distribute the moisture and contribute to the drying process taking place faster.

Always check and clear out excess lint from the lint tray before and after using the dryer. When this is not clear, the efficiency of the dryer can be reduced. This results in longer drying times. It can also cause the dryer to overheat and cause serious problems!

Sewing Clothes

Have you ever had to ditch your chosen outfit for the day because a button was missing? From now on, as long as you have a sewing needle and some matching thread, those days should be long behind you!

Before using any sewing tools, make sure that you're getting permission from a parent or guardian, and make sure to always double-check where you're placing your tools at all times for safety reasons.

Sewing a Button

Keep safe by keeping your needle in a place where you can see it at all times.

♥ Start by threading the needle and tying a knot at the end of the thread.

♥ Then, from the bottom side of where the button will be, push the sharp point of the needle through the material to the top side.

♥ At half the diameter of the button, push the needle down again so you have sewn a short strip.

If you will be sewing a button with two holes, use this short strip as an anchor.

♥ Place your button over the strip of thread and continue sewing with the needle as before.

♥ This time, when you push the needle from the bottom, it must go through the material and the first buttonhole.

♥ Pull the needle out and push it into the second buttonhole, then into the material below, where you will repeat the action.

♥ Do this about five times so your button is secure.

♥ Return the needle to the bottom side of the material and make a knot before cutting off the remainder of the thread.

If the button you are sewing on has four holes, your anchor thread should cross over to form an X.

♥ Place your button over this mark.

♥ Treat the four button holes as two pairs of two holes.

♥ Move the thread between the two pairs until the button is securely sewn on.

♥ Tie the knot on the back side of the material and cut the thread.

Sewing Ripped Clothes

♥ For a rip in your clothes, start by laying the garment flat on the table.

♥ Thread your needle and tie a knot at the end of it.

♥ From the bottom side of the fabric, bring your needle through to the top and loosely join the fabric together by using the thread to bring the matching edges of the material together.

♥ Then, move your thread to the bottom of the rip and carefully sew small parallel stitches all the way to the top of the rip.

Sewing on a Patch

♥ You can sew on a patch using a piece of cloth that is slightly bigger than the hole it will cover.

♥ Start by trimming around the hole with a pair of scissors to neaten it up.

♥ Place the patch on the bottom side of the fabric so its

pattern is facing up at the hole.

♥ Then, sew around the edge of the patch to fasten it securely in place.

♥ You can use a running stitch to create a neatly sewn patch from the bottom.

♥ If you want your patch to be visible, you can place it on the top side of the material.

♥ Sew neatly around the edge of the patch in a continuous whip stitch to help it stand out.

ASL (American Sign Language)

Sign language is a physical language that can help you communicate with others, so long as they recognize the same type of sign language as you. There are different types of sign languages, but for these examples, we are going to look at American sign language, which uses hand movements and facial expressions. Sign language can help you communicate with friends and family who might have a hearing impairment or might be non-verbal. Knowing how to communicate using sign language can also open up career opportunities for you, as it is a skill that is perhaps not as common as others and is a valuable asset to help a company's customers and employees!

Here are some great words to get started with:

Hello

♥ Bring your hand up so your fingers are in alignment with your brow and your palm is facing the person you are greeting.

♥ Let your thumb and little finger touch so that only the three inner fingers are standing.

♥ Now, move your hand away from the side of your brow in a sideways salute.

Thank You

♥ Bring your flat hand up so your fingers are covering your chin.

♥ Now, move your hand away from your chin toward the person you are talking to while mouthing the words "Thank you".

You're Welcome

You're Welcome

♥ Take a closed, flat hand up to your chin (as if you were measuring something that was at your chin's height).

♥ With a curving C motion, bring your flat hand down to your chest (as if there was an invisible bubble from your chin to chest)

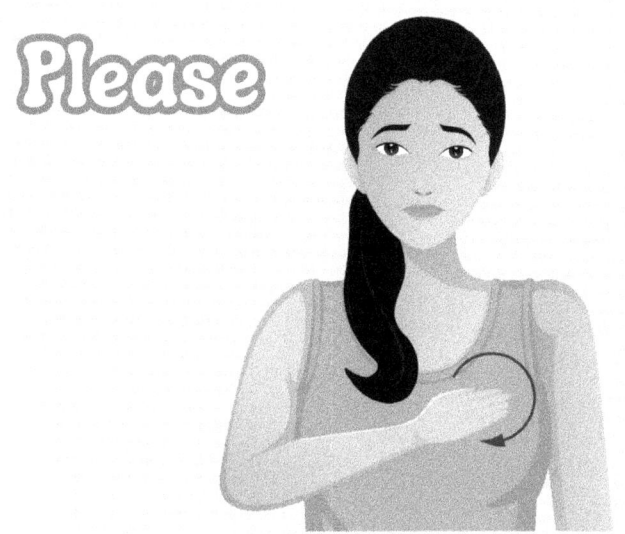

Please

♥ Place your right hand flat on the center of your chest.

♥ Move your hand clockwise, from left to right, a few times.

Yes

♥ Ball your hands into a forward-facing fist.

♥ Straighten and bend your wrist so your fist moves up and down in a nodding movement.

♥ You can also match the nod with your head as you are doing this.

CHAPTER FIVE

Tidy Life Skills

Cleaning, Decluttering, and Designing Your Cozy Creative Space!

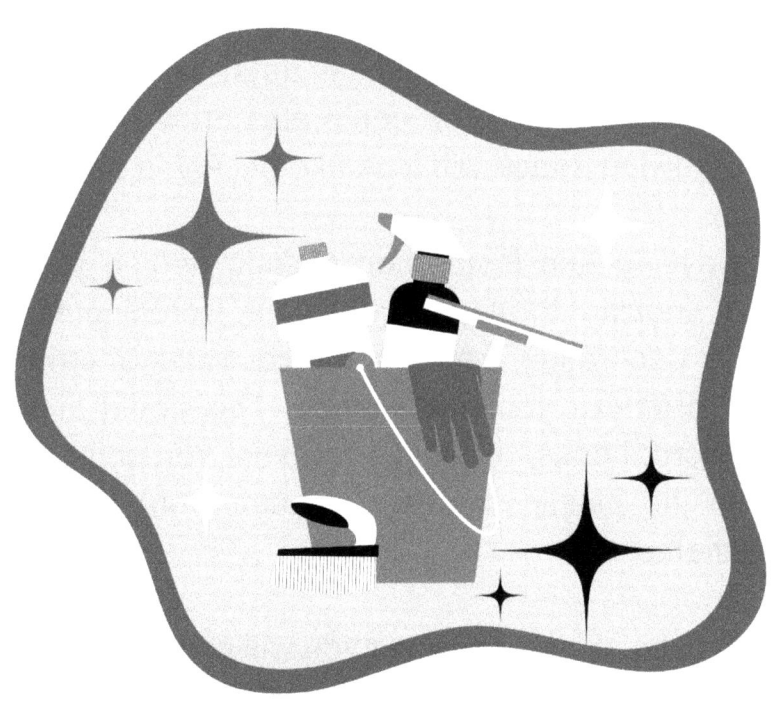

Living your most creative life is best done in a space that inspires creativity. This is an attractive space without clutter that inspires joy everywhere you look. This joy could be in the form of a well-organized bookshelf, a favorite poster, or the symmetry between your well-hung curtains and the rest of the furniture in your room!

Finding Your Inspo

Before you begin transforming your living space, imagine what you want it to look like. You've got to visualize your room before you can actualize the look of it. To help you with this, you can create an inspo collage using pictures from magazines or online sources. You can write down ideas in your journal, describing in detail what items you prefer in which areas. You could also draw a layout of what your living space will look like once you are done.

Other ways to find inspiration include finding a color scheme, looking through magazines, scrolling social media, or decorating around a theme. Think of creative ways to organize your belongings. This could include using Velcro, hooks, or plastic shelves. You could even decorate the plastic shelves to match your theme or color scheme.

Create a list of all the activities you will need to carry out to achieve your final vision. This list will serve as a plan to guide your steps throughout the process. You can cross items off the list as you accomplish them.

Your room needs to be a space where you can work with focus. Your mind will have difficulty focusing in a messy place. You need to clear out the distractions first, then bring in joy by creatively transforming your room into a space that appeals to your senses.

Declutter

The number of things you own may have accumulated over the years. Old toys, books, clothes, and other forgotten items may lie hidden at the back of your closet. It's time to let them go to make space for your new glowed-up look. Separate the things you use from those you want to discard. This creates space for new items and makes finding your stuff so much easier. (But remember, if something means a lot to you or feels nostalgic, don't get rid of it! If you don't want it in your room, then see where else you can store it neatly in your home.)

Your parents and/or guardians can help you gift your old items to new owners. Other children, such as younger siblings, relatives, neighbors, or even strangers who belong to an organization, are waiting for your donation. Your guardians can suggest the best ways to help you declutter by suggesting where these items can find a new home!

Declutter in a structured way. You can start with a small section at a time while integrating the KonMari method invented by Marie Kondo. If you break your room into four corners, you can finish decluttering by the end of the week. Set aside time to sort your items into the categories that the KonMari method suggests.

These categories are:

♥ clothes

♥ books

♥ papers

♥ miscellaneous items

♥ sentimental items or mementos

When following this approach, it's easier to decide which items are worth keeping or require letting go. Using this method ensures that decluttering is a once-off effort rather than a non-ending task. It will help minimize distractions from items that have not been sorted yet.

When you are sorting through your miscellaneous items, such as old bottles of shampoo, skincare products, and make-up, take time to look at the expiration dates; most people are not aware that these items have them! You can find them on the sides or bottom of the bottles or jars.

To find the expiration dates on your cosmetics, look for a sign that looks like an open jar. This is the PAO symbol, also known as the "period after opening." If you are having difficulty finding this sign, look next to the bar code and the manufacturer details. The number you will find written here is the number of months that the product can stay in use after you have first opened the bottle or container. Items, such as cosmetics that can stay in use for more than 30 months will have this POA sign on them. If products have a shelf life that is shorter than 30 months, then their expiration date will be indicated by a "best before" date.

Using cosmetics after these dates could have severe consequences, such as causing an allergic reaction when they touch your skin! This is because the chemical component of the item will have changed over time due to a breakdown in its chemical structure.

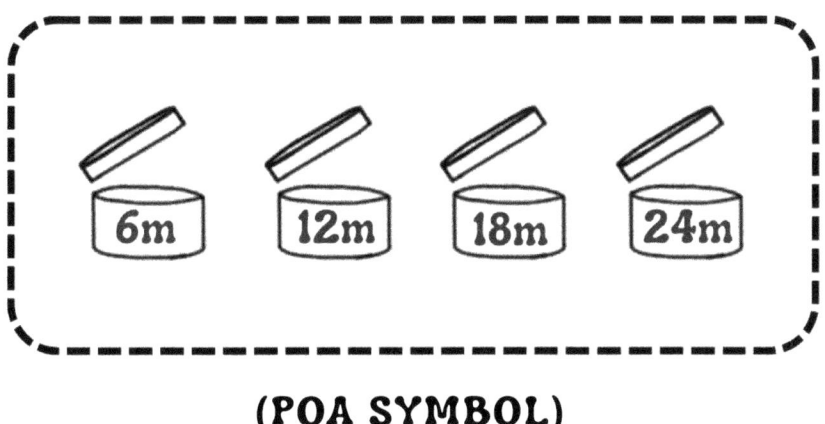

(POA SYMBOL)

Keep Loved Items

As you are getting rid of the items that you no longer make use of, carefully consider which items you will be keeping. The items that you hold on to should be those items that you absolutely love. Or, as Marie Kondo says, "Only keep the items that spark joy." This statement can guide you in throwing out those items you have no use for. As you are working through the different sections of items, it will be even more useful to further separate each category into sub-categories. So, for example, as you sort through your books, you may find journals, school textbooks, fiction books, non-fiction books, and magazines. Create different piles for these so you can easily identify which items to discard and which to keep!

Tidying, Cleaning, and Getting Cozy!

Now you have decluttered and made space, it's time to clean and get cozy! The brain has a hard time focusing when your environment is messy and disorganized, and this even has the power to reduce our brain's resources! The best way to start is by picking one area of your room to work on first.

You can start with the little things like:

♥ taking garbage to the trash can

♥ bringing any dirty dishes to the kitchen

♥ making your bed

♥ getting your laundry together

Once you take care of these things, you can start doing the finishing touches, like:

♥ vacuuming

♥ polishing

♥ cleaning mirrors and windows

♥ wiping down surfaces

It can be hard to get motivated to get started cleaning, so here are a few of my tips to get you in the mood:

♥ put on your favorite music

♥ just commit to getting 1 small thing done for a dopamine boost (trust me, even if you just get 1 small thing done, you will want to get more done and get in the flow!)

♥ watch some cleaning and decluttering videos you find online

Cleaning List

Daily
- ☐ _____
- ☐ _____
- ☐ _____
- ☐ _____

Weekly
- ☐ _____
- ☐ _____
- ☐ _____
- ☐ _____

Monthly
- ☐ _____
- ☐ _____
- ☐ _____
- ☐ _____

Decorating

Once you have finished cleaning up your space, you can start decorating it. Refer to your Inspo collage and the list you created when you started. This can help guide your process!

When decorating your room, keep in mind that this is your safe space, so think about all of the things that make you feel cozy and happy. This is the space that you can't wait to come home to! This means you will want to ultimately look to yourself for inspiration for how you want it to feel and look.

Creative Corner

A creative corner is a space where you can sit and do your work without being disturbed or distracted by anything that does not help you feel motivated or creative.

Ask yourself what makes you happy because you can shower this corner with everything that inspires you and brings about good vibes! If music makes you happy, then feature musical aspects in your personal space. This could come in the form of a poster of your favorite musical artist or creating a place where you can easily store and access your headphones. This creative corner can be a desk, it can be a cozy chair, and it can even be a blanket and some pillows surrounded by your favorite plushies!

Use Some Dopamine Decor

Do you ever feel that overwhelming tingly feeling of happiness when it's the last Friday before your school break and you know you're about to have a sleepover with your best friends, or you get to the last level of your video game, or a new season of your favorite show comes out? That's dopamine! Dopamine is the feel-good hormone that your brain releases when you feel happy. This feeling can motivate you to work better and to be more creative. Without dopamine, we can end up feeling uninspired and low instead of enjoying creating and contributing to a brighter world around us!

So why not create that same feeling with the decor that's in your space? This is called dopamine decor! Use dopamine decor in the spaces where you want to feel inspired. You can also use dopamine decor in places where you may need to do things that are boring and a chore to do. Dopamine decor could be as simple as replacing your regular lights with cool lava lamps and fairy lights. It can consist of really fun plushies that are huge instead of regular pillows or bean bags instead of chairs! It can even include transforming those plain white walls into works of art covered by posters, pictures, artwork, and notes!

Balance Your Mood With Colors

Different colors affect your mood in varying ways. Think about how you feel and compare it to how you would like to feel. Choose the color that will put you in the right mind space to be as creative as you can be!

Red is the color to use if you feel tired and need an energy boost. You can incorporate red by adding a cushion, adding some red frames to some of your pictures, or even changing your bed cover!

Orange is a color that can make you feel playful. It also brings joy and welcomes friendship. This may be a good color for the space where you like to spend time with your friends and family. They will feel welcome and happy when they are in that space with you.

Yellow is a color that increases your self-confidence. It is a good color to come home to after something has happened to make you doubt yourself. This color will make you happy and help you remember how awesome you are!

Pink is a good color to lift your self-esteem, especially when the darker shades of pink are used. On the other hand, the lighter shades of pink provide a nurturing feeling and can help you deal with feelings of loneliness.

Green can calm you down if you feel stressed, like the way you sometimes feel before a test. After spending some time in your green space, you will feel rejuvenated and ready to tackle the world. The mood-lifting effect works best when you use lighter shades of green.

Blue is another stress-busting color. This color reminds us of the cloudless sky and has a calming effect. If you use darker tones of blue, it will help you improve your ability to focus.

Purple is a cool color for your yoga and meditation corner. It will encourage you to be spiritually aware. It will also encourage you to think deeply about things. If there is a problem that you cannot quite figure out, this can be the corner where you go to find solutions. It can also be a good place to reflect on the day, as purple helps with deep thinking.

When your living space looks cozy and welcoming, it will make you feel good. This is due to the effect of dopamine and other hormones that are released into your system to help regulate your mood. This is good for your mental well-being. Living in a physical space that makes you happy will result in you feeling inspired every day!

Now that you have decided on the colors you will use to bring the spark into your room, add some of the decorative elements you added to your list earlier. These will help bring the color in. They can be items such as sparkles, posters, candles, flowers, cushions, picture frames, book ends, fairy lights, and pinboards. If you need some inspiration, you can look through magazines, check out Pinterest, find websites that focus on decor, or visit the decor aisle in your local general store. If you enjoy artistic projects, you may use this inspiration to build your own decor, such as picture frames and pinboards. You will need the help of some paint, glue, and other items that can be used to express your creative decorating self!

Have fun with the process, and you will soon have a space that is so comfortable that you will enjoy spending time working and creating in it!

CHAPTER SIX

Money Life Skills

**Investing, Banking, Budgeting, and Finance Hacks
Most Adults Wished They Knew!**

It's been said that money makes the world go round. If that is true, then the best thing to stop you from falling off the merry-go-round is to know how to manage it well! That's what this chapter is all about. You'll learn all about how to manage your money, investing tips (that most adults don't even know!), the different types of accounts that exist, how to choose the best account for your needs, how to plan your budget, and a bunch more!

Keeping Your Money Safe

When your parents and/or guardians give you money to spend, they can provide it to you in different forms. They could give you cash. This happens when they give you $10 in hand for you to go and buy something around the corner. They could also decide to open a bank account on your behalf, so you'll have access to plastic. By plastic, I am referring to a bank card that provides an easy way for you to access funds when you need them. It is safer to carry than dollar bills because if you lose your bag, all your cash could go with it. With a bank card, you only need to get a replacement card. However, if you ever lose your bank card, remember to ask the bank to freeze it so nobody else can use it. You can even do this through the bank's mobile app!

To open a bank account, you need your parents and/or guardians to help you. If you want to open a bank account independently, you will usually need to wait until you are 18 years old, depending on your circumstances. There are two different types of cards you could be given:

Debit Cards

A debit card is a card that lets you use money that is already sitting in your account that you deposited earlier.

Credit Cards

A credit card allows you to borrow money from the bank by promising to pay it back later. The bank will give you a limit to how much you are allowed to borrow until it is paid back. You can use this borrowed money whenever you need it, but just remember that you will need to pay off at least some of the money you have borrowed each month! The bank will have something called a monthly minimum, which is the amount that you will need to pay off that month. But super-responsible borrowers will pay off their cards in full every month!

Often, when credit is paid back, you need to pay it back with interest. This means that even though you may have used $10 on your credit card, when you pay it back, you may have to pay back $10.10. The amount that you will have to pay back to the bank after using the credit card is called interest or APR (annual percentage rate). Its amount depends on the agreement that was made when the credit card was first given to you. In the above example, 10% interest needs to be paid back in addition to the initial borrowed amount. Think of interest as you saying, "Thank you, bank, here is an extra $0.10 for being so kind as to let me borrow money up front!"

ATM Usage

You can use your debit card or credit card to withdraw money at an ATM (automated teller machine). The amount that you can withdraw depends on how much is available in your account. With both types of cards, you will need a PIN (personal identification number) to withdraw money from the ATM. A PIN is a secret number that only you know, that is linked to your card and gives you access to the funds. Make sure nobody else sees your PIN number while you are typing it in at an ATM, as they could then access your money if they managed to get hold of your card!

Checking Account vs Savings Accounts

Think of a checking account as your go-to account for

daily use, like purchases, withdrawing money, automatic deposits from your job, etc. A checking account is usually the one that has a debit card linked to it. So when you use your debit card, the money comes right out of your checking account!

Think of a savings account as a piggy bank that you want to grow over time to have funds in case of emergencies or for saving up for large purchases, like a car one day, etc.

Checks

Checks are linked to your checking account. They provide an alternative way to withdraw money from your account other than using a debit card.

Somebody could write a check out to you for a specific amount. When you redeem the check at the bank, you are asking the bank to give you the money that is equivalent to the amount written on the check.

If you write out a check, you need to write down whom the check is being made out to. This should be written "cash" if it is a cash check. Otherwise, write it out in the name of the person to whom you are giving the money. Write out the full amount of the check in words. This must include the full dollar amount and the full cents amount. The check also has space for writing the amount in numbers. The number value and the word value of the check need to be the same. You will need to date the check and sign it. When the check recipient cashes or deposits the check to redeem it, your bank will compare the signature on the check against the version of your signature they keep on file. They will also confirm that there is enough money in your account to cover the amount of money that they will pay out. Once they are satisfied that the check is genuine, they will release the funds for payment to the person presenting the check.

When you present a check, the bank tellers will give you money in exchange for the check. If you want, you can deposit the check into your account. In this case, instead of withdrawing the cash from the account of the person who wrote the check, you will be requesting that the bank transfer the value of the check into your bank account.

Once the money has been deposited or transferred into your bank account, you may use it! You can use it by swiping your debit card, withdrawing the money at an ATM, or withdrawing the money from the bank by asking a bank teller for assistance.

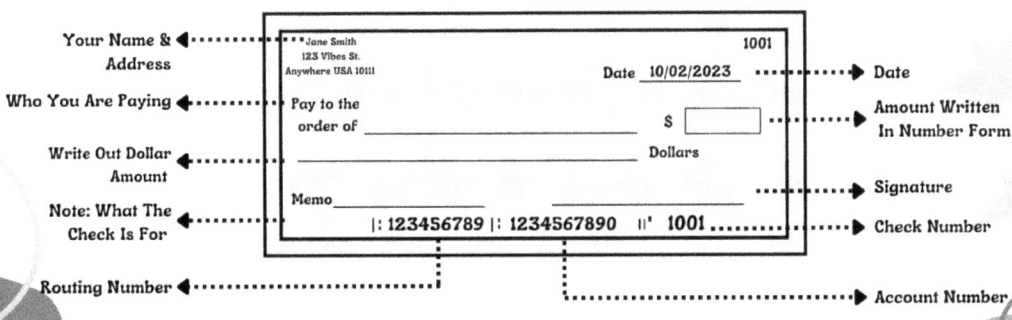

Money Orders

Money orders are a safe way to send and receive money anywhere in the world. You can access these services through an outlet such as Western Union, MoneyGram, or your local post office. The money is sent via wire transfer to the location of your choosing. You need to be over 18 years old to use the service. Therefore, you will need assistance from your parents and/or guardians should you need to send or receive money using this option. Sending money requires the senders' Social Security number, the amount of money that needs to be transferred, and their contact details.

If you have a bank checking account that was opened with the assistance of your parents or guardians, you can access the services via your local bank branch. Your banker will transfer the funds from your account to wherever you want to send them!

The person who is going to receive the money will receive a message via text or email to alert them that the money has arrived! Using the reference number from the message, they can go to their local outlet to withdraw the money. They will need to carry their personal identification document to confirm that they are the true recipient of the money. This will allow the bank to securely hand the money over to them. If the person you are sending the money to is under 18, they will need a guardian to assist them with withdrawing the money.

(Money Order Example)

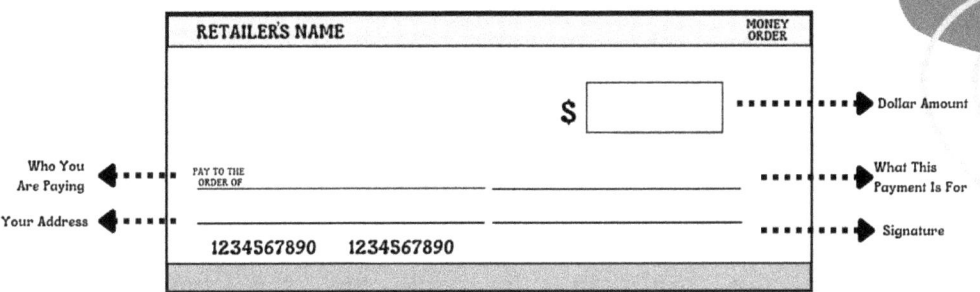

Planning for the Future

Saving

By being smart and not spending all your money on things you want upfront (like makeup, bowling, clothes, etc.), you can put it aside to grow over time! This is known as saving. Try saving a percentage of your birthday, holiday, or chore money and putting it into your savings account or piggy bank! Having a set number percentage, like 20%, especially for your savings, will help you stay on track. Saving money in this way can also help you with smaller opportunities, like your favorite singer playing a concert in town and needing expensive tickets, to more long-term purchases, like buying your first car one day! This is a grown-up way of showing your family and friends that you are responsible and good with money and planning!

Budgeting

Budgeting is when you plan what you will spend your money on in the future. Usually, to stay on track, people will budget their finances on a monthly basis. Budgeting ensures that you have enough money to spend on what you want by knowing what each item costs beforehand. Simply put, budgeting is really about arranging what money comes in and what money goes out. You'll need to prioritize your expenses. As a tween, it may be as simple as making sure you have enough snack money for school and fun activities on the weekends while making sure you are bringing in enough chore money! A good example of smart budgeting would be going to see that movie at an earlier time so a ticket is cheaper, and this way, you will have enough money left over for the arcade!

Can you think of any monthly items or activities you need to budget for? Use this next work sheet to help you keep track by when, how, and what you earn and spend!

Checks & Balances
Tracker

Date	Description	Money Earned +	Money Spent −	Balance

Total Saved:

Investing

Investing is basically about growing your money, usually for the long term. Instead of putting all of your money into your savings account, you can put some of it into a special investment account. These accounts are known as exchanges. They look just like regular bank accounts and have their own mobile apps, etc, but you can buy stocks and bonds with them (more on this later!). Some apps that you may consider using for your investments include Robinhood, Fidelity, and Vanguard.

When you invest for the long term, it's good to think about what you want your life and money to look like 10, 20, or 50 years from today. Think of investing $10 today, and in many years, it could be worth $100. It's the money equivalent of growing a seedling into a giant oak tree over time!

If you start investing your money as soon as possible, then the amount you invest will grow a lot more because it has more time to grow. Money growing over time is called compounding! What this means is that every month, you will earn interest (money) on the invested amount. You will also earn interest on the previous month's interest and all the months before that. This is known as compound interest. These amounts accrue, which means that they add up. So the only thing you need to remember is the more money you invest and the sooner you do it, the better!

Your Investment Goal

One of my favorite things to do is dream about my investment goals! Do you want to have your monthly bills paid for automatically by dividends (money getting paid to you for the stocks you own!) when you grow up? Do you want to retire with 1 million dollars? All of these things are possible with a clever investment goal and plan! You can ask your parents and/or guardians to help you open an investment account to get started.

Bonds

Basically, a bond is a way of letting someone borrow some of your money for a specified amount of time, and then, when that time is up, they will pay you money on top of what they borrowed to say thank you! Bonds are not a physical item that arrives at your house, but more like a deal you make. Bonds are usually thought of as being safe investments because you are guaranteed to get the "thank you" money that was agreed on. For example, if you bought a bond for $100 that pays you 10% interest after 5 years, then the bond will pay you back your $100 with an extra $10, so $110 in total. And you basically made $10 without having to work. That's making your money work for you!

Stocks

Just like bonds, stocks aren't physical items that show up at your house when you buy them! When you buy a stock of a company, it basically means that you own a teeny tiny piece of that company! For example, if you bought a stock of your favorite makeup brand for $100, then if the company was doing really well, your stock might go up in price to, say, $110, but if they weren't doing so well, then your stock might go down in price to, say, $50! See how stocks are a little more dangerous in terms of losing your money than bonds but also have a higher chance of making you more money at the same time? When people call stocks "volatile." they mean that you could lose your money easily! Stocks are a great way to make lots of money over time! If you would have bought a bunch of Amazon stock 10 years ago, then now you would be mega-rich because that company is doing so well! You make your money on stocks when you finally sell them for more than you originally bought them for, and then you can put that money back into your regular bank account if you need to. But make sure to hold on to well-performing stocks for a long time because companies can really grow over the years, and your stocks grow in value along with them! You can also sell your stocks whenever you would like if they are not performing well.

ETFs

If you can't pick what companies to invest in, then you can buy what's called an ETF (exchange-traded fund). This is a tiny piece of a bunch of companies all condensed into one super-stock! ETFs are considered pretty safe because when one of the companies in an ETF is not performing well, another one might be doing great!

Dividends

In order to say "thank you" for buying their stocks and to make their stocks more appealing, some companies will pay out what's called a dividend. A dividend is usually a set amount that the company will pay quarterly (this means every 3 months!) to anyone who owns their stock. Having lots of dividend-paying stocks will mean that you will make money just by owning them! Making money like this without having to work is called passive income. Ahh, ain't that the life?!

Keeping Your Investments Safe!

It's really good to diversify your investments. Diversifying means making sure you have lots of different types of investments instead of just one stock. This is safer because if you have all of your money in one stock, then if that company goes bankrupt, you will lose your money!

You may have heard people use the term "investment portfolio." Your portfolio simply means all of your different types of investments all put together, like stocks, ETFs, bonds, etc. It's good practice to buy stocks from different types of companies and not just from a single industry. An example of this would be to own some stocks in technology companies, but also some in energy companies (known as commodities), some in entertainment companies, and so on! The more diverse your portfolio (investments you have), the safer your money is!

Making Money

Even though you are below the official employment age, you can still find ways to earn money! Learning how to make and manage your money now will empower you with skills you can use for the rest of your life!

To make extra money, talk to your parents and/or guardians, extended family members, and trusted neighbors. Offer to help out with chores for money, but make sure that the time these extra chores take does not negatively impact your school work or other responsibilities!

Aside from letting people know that you are available for extra chores, you can also approach people directly with suggestions. For example, say if your neighbor is your parent's best friend and is having problems raking leaves from their lawn, you can offer to spend an afternoon doing it for them in exchange for payment!

Other activities that you could do in exchange for money include:

♥ dog walking for family, friends, and neighbors

♥ babysitting for a few hours

♥ sorting the laundry and putting it in the washer and dryer, then folding it

♥ selling handmade items like jewelry, artwork, or hand-painted T-shirts

In each instance, discuss the available options with your parents or guardians first. This way, they can advise you and keep in touch with you to ensure your safety at all times. If there are other skills you have that can be exchanged for money, write these down and try to approach some potential customers, so long as you and your family know and trust them. The joy and freedom of earning your own money will make you feel so empowered and ready to tackle the world!

CHAPTER SEVEN

Health Life Skills

The Healthy Girl's Guide to Fitness, Sleep, Hydration, and Diet!

Keeping healthy is good for you on so many levels. Health is one way that your glow-up shows on the outside. It also impacts every other aspect of your life; keep it healthy so you can function at your best level!

By keeping fit and healthy both inside and outside, you will have radiant-looking skin, hair, nails, and a healthy body. When your body functions optimally, it will release endorphins (feel-good hormones) that result in you naturally feeling amazing. This reduces the likelihood of symptoms of anxiety and depression!

Healthy Eating

Your diet can have long-term effects on your body! The impact of healthy or unhealthy food and drink choices will slowly start to determine what your body looks like and your resilience to disease. For example, drinking water over fizzy drinks will help you feel healthy and improve your body's ability to digest food and flush out toxins. Drinking water encourages your skin to look healthy and glow. Conversely, fizzy drinks and greasy food are difficult for the body to flush out. As a result, you could experience high blood sugar levels, worsened health conditions, and acne. Choosing fruit and vegetables over junk food will have the opposite affect and leave you feel amazing!

Making Healthy Choices

When was the last time you read the nutrition label on the back of your chips? You know all those crazy ingredients? Well, if you can't pronounce them, then you probably shouldn't be putting them in your body! I know we all love some junk foods from time to time, but it's important to be aware of the nasty ingredients in some of these processed foods that are poisonous to your body in the long term. Chemicals such as nitrates, potassium bromate, artificial colors, BHT, and BHA can cause the growth of cells that you do not want in your system! Hormones can also be affected negatively. There is usually a healthier version of your favorite foods that don't contain unnecessary food dye or chemicals that you can find in supermarkets if you look in the health foods section! Share the things that you learn about nutrition with your family so you can all make healthy choices together!

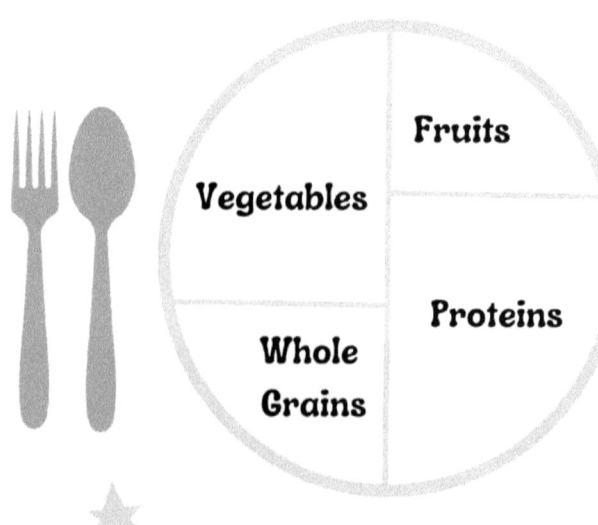

Reading Food Labels

The labels on food items will give you the expiration date, AKA the "best before" date. Avoid eating or drinking expired products, as they could be poisonous due to changes in their chemical composition!

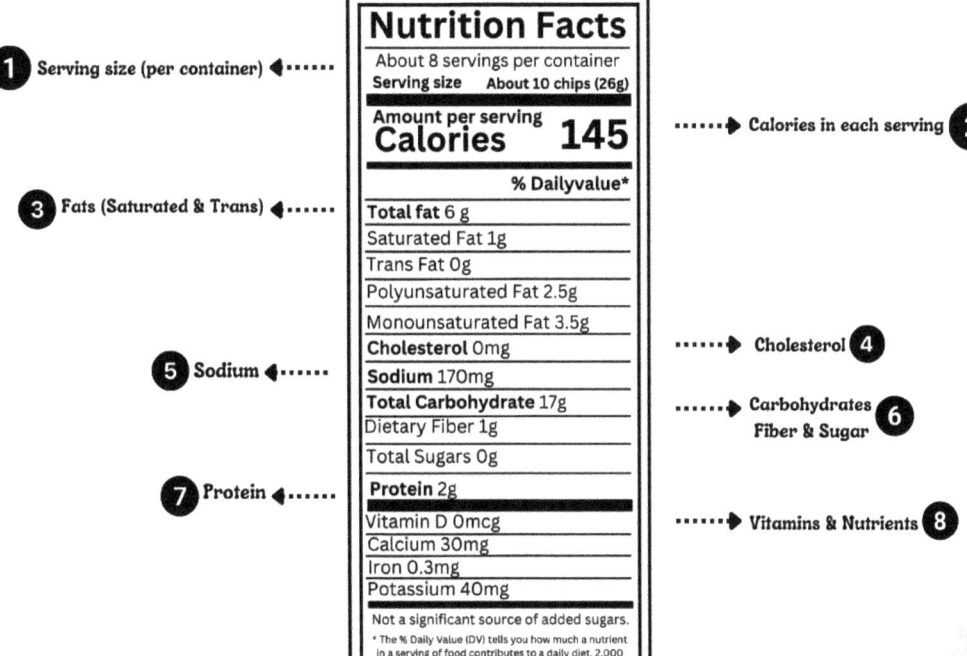

1 Serving size (per container)

2 Calories in each serving

3 Fats (Saturated & Trans)

4 Cholesterol

5 Sodium

6 Carbohydrates Fiber & Sugar

7 Protein

8 Vitamins & Nutrients

Nutrition Facts

About 8 servings per container

Serving size About 10 chips (26g)

Amount per serving
Calories 145

% Dailyvalue*

Total fat 6 g	
Saturated Fat 1g	
Trans Fat 0g	
Polyunsaturated Fat 2.5g	
Monounsaturated Fat 3.5g	
Cholesterol 0mg	
Sodium 170mg	
Total Carbohydrate 17g	
Dietary Fiber 1g	
Total Sugars 0g	
Protein 2g	
Vitamin D 0mcg	
Calcium 30mg	
Iron 0.3mg	
Potassium 40mg	

Not a significant source of added sugars.

* The % Daily Value (DV) tells you how much a nutrient in a serving of food contributes to a daily diet. 2,000 calories a day is used for general nutrition advice.

1. Serving Information: Serving information on nutritional labels usually estimates the amount of servings in each food package. For example, in this container, there are 8 servings, and each serving amounts to 10 chips. Meaning that there will be approximately 80 chips in the bag.

2. Calories: Calories are the amount of energy released in your body when consumed. In this example, a serving (10 chips) is 145 calories. (So keep that in mind because a whole bag would amount to 1,160 calories!).

3. Fats: Our bodies do need a certain amount of fats each day, but too much can be bad for our health! This label signifies how much fat you will get per serving (10 chips).

4. Cholesterol: Did you know that your liver actually produces cholesterol itself? But you can also get it from animal-based foods. You will want to stay within the daily range of your cholesterol.

5. Sodium: Sodium is one of the chemical components found in salt. Although some people think that sodium means table salt, they are not actually the same thing. As many processed foods contain a lot of sodium, it is best to eat them sparingly. However, our bodies do need a small amount of sodium to function.

6. Carbohydrates, Fiber, & Sugar: Most nutritional labels will cover the three main types of carbohydrates, which are fiber, sugar, and starch. Carbohydrates, more commonly known as carbs, are also a source of energy, and our bodies use them for lots of important jobs like regulating our blood glucose.

7. Protein: Protein is a super important part of our daily diet! Not only is it another energy source, but our bodies use protein to build muscle cells and even to repair our bones!

8. Vitamins & Nutrients: Vitamins and nutrients are the foundational elements towards staying healthy. They work to boost your immune system, which protects you from getting sick, and they help your organs and cells do their job properly! Sometimes, you can have too many vitamins and nutrients, so nutritional labels are a useful tool to help you keep track.

Hydration Station

Everyone is always going on about how we should drink enough water and stay hydrated, but why is that? Well, it turns out that water is pretty important! Here are some benefits of staying hydrated:

♥ Helps acne and boosts skin's health and beauty

♥ flushes out toxins

♥ avoids kidney damage

♥ lubricates your joints

♥ helps digestive system work properly

♥ helps regulate body temperature (essential for summer activities)

♥ creates layer of protection for your spinal cord, brain, and other really important tissues

♥ helps breathing (water keeps your airways open, keeping asthma and allergies from getting worse!)

♥ and so many more!

Did you know that your recommended daily water intake changes as you get older?! Between the ages of 9 and 13, you should aim to drink 5 to 6 glasses of water per day. From ages 14 to 18, you can increase your daily water intake to 6 to 8 glasses.

Here are some really easy ways to remember to stay hydrated and keep track of how much water you're drinking:

♥ If you have a phone, you can set alarm reminders

♥ Download a water reminder app

♥ Get a really cute water bottle that makes you excited! (I know this sounds silly, but I noticed myself drinking more water when I bought myself a glittery bottle and put my favorite stickers on it!)

♥ Use the water tracker in this book! (You don't need any apps; you can use a paper water tracker like the one on the next page!)

Weekly
Water Tracker

Monday							
Tuesday							
Wednesday							
Thursday							
Friday							
Saturday							
Sunday							

Food Groups

There are five food group categories to consider when determining whether or not you are eating a balanced diet. These are fruits, vegetables, proteins, dairy, and grains.

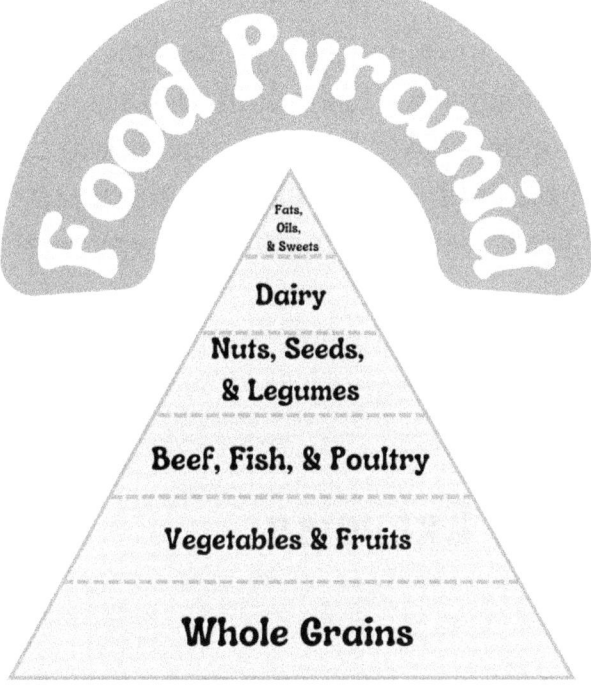

♥ Grains are foods in their seed form, like rice, wheat, oats, and barley. They can be whole like rice and oats or ground like flour.

♥ Dairy refers to milk products like cream and cheese.

♥ Protein can be found in meat, such as poultry, beef, and mutton. Fish, beans, and nuts are also a good source of protein.

♥ Fruit is great for your digestive system because of its healthy fiber! Try and eat five servings a day

♥ Vegetables contain a whole world of benefits for the body! Consume darker-colored vegetables for increased nutrients.

This will vary from person to person depending on allergies, sensitivities, personal dietary choices, and personal health conditions, so make sure to consult your doctor and parents or guardians to make sure that your diet is balanced with any restrictions you might have!

If you are having a hard time eating the recommended amount of fruit and veggies, then why not try blending a yummy smoothie?!

Consistent Exercise

Benefits

Regular exercise benefits your body by reducing the amount of stress and tension you experience. This can help you focus when you need to study or engage in any activity that requires your full attention. Reduced tension can also improve your sleep quality, as you will have less to worry about and, therefore, fall asleep more easily. Worrying less reduces the likelihood of suffering from anxiety or depression. Instead, the hormones released during exercise can increase the joy you feel as enthusiasm for exercise and other activities is increased.

Exercise helps improve your fitness level. By challenging your body, you can improve your self-image. Be careful not to over-exercise, though, as this can impact negatively on your current growth spurt or lead to too much weight loss.

When you exercise, do it to stay fit and healthy rather than to look good. Exercise will benefit you both now and well into adulthood. This happens because it increases bone mass, reduces blood pressure, lowers blood cholesterol, and increases muscle strength. While these benefits will help you to be a better athlete now, when you are older, they can help you have a better-managed aging process.

Types of Exercise

Different types of exercise impact different systems in your body. By putting pressure on these body systems, you strengthen them over time.

♥ Cardiovascular exercise impacts your heart and the flow of blood through your body. Also known as cardio or aerobic exercise, this kind of exercise helps improve lung capacity and lowers blood pressure and blood sugar levels. This mood-boosting exercise is a good option to engage in for burning fat and lowering cholesterol levels. Types of cardio or cardiovascular exercise include aerobics, running, cycling, and dancing.

♥ Strength training exercises impact your muscle strength directly. It helps improve your body posture and balance. In the long run, this type of exercise helps regulate blood sugar levels and increases bone density. Lifting weights with a trainer at the gym, doing squats, and using resistance bands are types of strength training.

♥ Stretching helps maintain muscle tone. It improves flexibility, reducing the likelihood of muscle cramps. It is beneficial to do some stretches before aerobic exercises to help reduce muscle strain. Rotating your joints and pulling your limbs in directions that are different from regular directional use helps to stretch muscles and tendons.

♥ Balance exercises help maintain balance and improve muscle and tendon strength. Balance exercises include trying to maintain balance while standing in irregular positions. These include tests such as standing on one leg without toppling over. Some yoga and dance exercises improve your ability to balance.

Enjoyable Workouts

When workouts are enjoyable, you will tend to do them more. To make this aspect of your health something that you enjoy rather than dread, try an exercise method that suits your personality! Here are a few examples to help you choose what could work for you:

Dance

Hip-hop, ballet, and Zumba are all dance exercises. You can sign up for these or widen your scope and discover dance moves that get your blood flowing!

Group Exercise

Set up a time with your friends when you can exercise together. This can involve either cardio or strength exercises. You can help each other improve your form so you do not strain your tendons. At the same time, exercising as a group encourages members to maintain consistency. Looking forward to spending time with friends is a good motivator on those days when you feel that you don't have the inner strength to get your gym clothes on!

New Skills

Kickboxing and karate are vigorous workouts that have the additional benefit of teaching you some self-defense moves. Find out if there are any classes in your neighborhood so you can engage your body's core and kick up some sweat!

Muscle Stretching

Exercises like yoga and Pilates do not involve a lot of cardiovascular activity. However, they help you develop muscle tone, flexibility, and mindfulness.

Water Sports

Swimming laps in the pool can build muscle tone and improve your heart and lung capacity. It also opens up avenues for new sports, like water gymnastics, underwater hockey, and water volleyball!

Online Classes

If you don't have access to a fitness center, you can join an online class. You will find that online classes are available for everything you would like to try your hand at. You can experiment in the comfort of your home while learning from an expert!

Safe Workouts

To avoid dehydration, remember to drink water to replenish what you sweat out! If you are really working up a sweat with a serious workout, like running long distances, you will want to replenish your electrolytes (minerals in your body that have an electric charge).

Electrolytes that help your cells function properly under stressful conditions can be found in some sports drinks!

Make sure to wear the appropriate exercise gear that will maintain the right body temperature and allow flexibility of movement. Shoes are also so important, especially when running!

Be gentle with your body. Stretch your muscles before your workout so you do not hurt yourself. Do not push yourself too much at the beginning of a new exercise regimen. Rather, work slowly toward your intended intensity. If you feel tired or ill, take a few days off from exercising until you are fully recovered. Exercising while you are ill could worsen your illness!

Getting Enough Sleep

Sleep is important for both your physical and mental well-being. During this tween stage of your life, you need between 8 to 10 hours of sleep. This provides your body with the boost it needs to engage fully in the coming day's activities.

While you are sleeping at night, your body replenishes itself. It repairs broken cells and produces enzymes and hormones. Some of the hormones that are activated include the growth hormone that causes your body to grow taller!

Improving Sleep Quality

There are a few things you can do to improve your sleep quality. These include:

♥ Maintain a sleep routine by having a set time for getting into bed every night. Provide adequate time for you to get at least eight hours of sleep. Avoid staying in bed beyond your regular waking up time and going to bed late during the weekend. This can negatively impact your weekday sleep schedule!

♥ Stay away from electronic devices for an hour before bedtime. Avoid staring at a screen before bed. They use blue light for their displays that trick your brain into thinking that it is daytime. Instead of screen time, do activities like reading, gentle yoga, or listening to chill music that will soothe your body so you get sleepy.

♥ Include some physical activity in your daytime routine to help you get rid of excess energy so you are tired enough to sleep at night.

♥ Expose yourself to daytime sunlight, especially in the morning. This will help regulate your internal body clock.

♥ Use blackout curtains. The presence of light in your bedroom while you are trying to sleep can disrupt your circadian rhythm (body clock), and your body can be confused if it's day or night. Your body needs to detect that it is nighttime to shut down properly for sleep!

♥ Regulate nighttime temperature. Temperature impacts your sleep! The best temperature for sleeping is about 65 degrees Fahrenheit. So, try to keep your bedroom cool, especially during the summer. Ask your parents and/or guardians to manage the thermostat at night so it is at the best temperature for sleeping. If the temperature is too hot, your body directs energy to cool your body down. When this happens, you end up tossing and turning!

CHAPTER EIGHT

Self-Care Life Skills

**Treat Yourself With Skincare, Haircare, & Hygiene Hacks
(You Deserve It!)**

You have got to love that fresh-faced look! But more than looking fresh is smelling and feeling fresh. That way, anybody who comes a little closer to interacting with that freshness will find that it permeates your being. Paying attention to your hygiene at this time in your life is ultra important. The introduction of new hormones into your body results in changes in physical structure, body odor, skin texture, and hair length. So, while you are coping with the psychological effects of discovering the changes within you, looking after your body for that continued freshness is something you also need to keep up with. A routine is key!

Skin

Cleansing Ritual

♥ As a first step, it's good to use a gentle cleanser that is free of any fragrance and chemicals and is hypoallergenic.

♥ Pat your face dry with a clean towel. Make sure the towel is clean to avoid any transfer of bacteria to your newly cleaned skin.

♥ The next step involves toning your skin with a toner that will minimize the appearance of open pores.

♥ And finally, hydrate your skin by using a moisturizer that is suitable for your skin type.

Different skin types include combination skin, dry skin, oily skin, normal, and sensitive. While dry and oily skin is self-explanatory, combination skin is dry in some areas and oily in others. The oily parts are usually over the nose, chin, cheekbones, and forehead; this is known as the T-Zone. Sensitive skin reacts easily to exposure to the elements and harsh skin care products. Normal skin tends to be evenly toned and can be cleaned using regular face cleansing products. Pay attention to how different products affect your skin; you know yourself best! Stop using a product if it negatively impacts your skin, and use ones that treat your skin well instead!

Exfoliate

Exfoliate your skin once a week to get rid of dead skin cells. Not removing these can result in a buildup of skin cells that can clog your pores. Clogged pores are the precursor to red blotches and acne. It's better to get in front of this problem by exfoliating once a week and avoiding needing to treat these skin problems in the long run.

If you do not have immediate access to an exfoliator, you can make your own. Use a spoonful of ground oatmeal mixed with a teaspoon of water. Rub this gently into your face and allow it to sit for 10 minutes while you meditate or try a new yoga pose. Once it is dried, you can rinse it off and pat your skin dry before moisturizing.

Sun Protection

When you go outside on a sunny day, protect your skin from overexposure to the sun. Not protecting your skin can lead to sunburn and dry skin. Dried skin is more likely to peel and flake off, resulting in uneven skin tone during the recovery period. Dry skin can also result in the development of acne. Use sunscreen with a sun protection factor (SPF) of 15 or higher to counter the effects of the sun.

When choosing a sunblock, be careful of ingredients that can disrupt hormonal development. This is especially important during this critical phase of your life when your hormones are developing and changing. The wrong sunscreen has the potential to impact negatively on the natural development of your body. The chemicals in some sunscreens enter the bloodstream through the skin and linger there. They can have long-lasting effects on your body. To be safe, avoid sunscreens with the following ingredients:

♥ avobenzone

♥ oxybenzone

♥ homosalate

♥ octisalate

♥ octocrylene

♥ octinoxate (octyl methoxycinnamate)

Once you have chosen a safe sunscreen or natural alternative, make sure you apply it to the parts of your skin that will be exposed to the sun. If you are in the sun for longer than two hours, reapply the sunscreen. Wearing sun hats with large brims will not only look cute but will also add additional protection for your face! If you couple this with a loose-fitting, long-sleeved shirt, you are less likely to be affected by sunburn.

In addition to cleansing and moisturizing your skin, keep it hydrated by drinking a lot of water and eating water-rich foods, such as cucumbers and watermelons. Avoid eating fast food and food made with a lot of grease, as this will eventually contribute to oily skin.

Skin Problems

The pores of your skin contain tiny hair follicles. These follicles contain glands that secrete an oily substance called sebum. This moisturizes the shafts of hair that grow out of the follicles. However, if the hair shaft is blocked, the sebum has challenges reaching the surface of the skin. Instead of getting excreted on the surface of the skin where you can wash away the oil, it gets stuck on the way out. Here, alongside the hair follicle, the sebum will mix with dead skin cells and form a bump just below the skin. This bump looks like a pimple, acne, a blackhead, or a whitehead. The type of bump that is formed is dependent on the location of the sebum.

Blackheads, Whiteheads, and Acne

♥ If the sebum is located along the follicle shaft, where it is exposed to oxygen from the air, it oxidizes and turns black. Then, it becomes a blackhead.

♥ If it is located under the skin, where it does not become oxidized, it remains white. This is known as a whitehead.

♥ If this bump, called a comedone, is not treated, it has the potential to erupt. When it erupts, the contents spread into surrounding skin cells. The sebum and dead skin cells mix with bacteria that naturally occur on the surface of skin cells. The combined presence of blackheads, whiteheads, and pimples is known as acne.

♥ This inflammation can also result in the formation of cysts, pustules, papules, or nodules.

♥ Papule is a different name for a pimple or a zit. It is a raised red bump on the skin. If it becomes pus-filled, then it will develop into a pustule.

♥ Pustules are filled with pus. They can be caused by insect bites, food allergies, or an allergic reaction to something in the environment.

♥ Cysts are inflamed and filled with liquid or air and look like blisters. They can form in any part of the body.

♥ Nodules are lumps that are firm to the touch. They can be found on the skin or within bodily tissue. When they are found in the skin, they develop at a deeper level of the skin than regular pimples do. They can be caused by viruses, bacteria, hormones, swollen lymph nodes, thyroid deficiency, or excess tissue growth. If you suspect that a lump or bump below the surface of your skin is a nodule, consult a doctor so they can make sure that it's not anything to worry about!

Treatment

To reduce the appearance of acne, wash your face twice a day using a mild cleanser or soap. Make sure that you thoroughly remove any makeup before going to bed so the pores of your skin can breathe. If the acne is also found on the skin of your chest and back, it is a good idea to consult with a dermatologist. They may prescribe medicine to help clear the acne.

If you have blackheads or whiteheads, avoid squeezing these, as it could lead to the formation of scars. Rather, stick to your daily cleansing regimen that includes toning. This will keep your skin clear. You could also use a face mask to lift excess dirt off your face.

Papules on the face can be treated with localized application of benzoyl peroxide, sulfur, or salicylic acid.

These over-the-counter treatments can be applied to individual pimples. When breakouts are severe, it is best to consult a dermatologist who can prescribe appropriate medication!

New Hair

With the move to adolescence, you will notice that hair starts to grow under your armpits and around your groin. Everyone is different; some girls may have thicker or darker hair on body parts like their belly, back, toes, face, chest, etc. Some girls may have one or more of these areas growing hair, and some girls might not have any. Some girls might even be really good at hiding it or getting rid of it, so don't ever feel negatively about growing hair anywhere on your body because it happens to EVERYBODY! Choosing whether or not to shave this new hair is a choice only you can make for yourself. Don't allow others to pressure you into it!

Shaving

If you choose to shave something like your legs or armpits (and, of course, with permission), here are some steps you can follow:

♥ Moisturize the area with soapy water to make it easier to shave

♥ Use a new gentle razor to help avoid cuts

♥ Shave in the direction that the hair is growing. This helps to reduce ingrown hair

♥ Wash with soap and water when you have finished. Dry your skin and use a gentle moisturizer to replace the moisture lost during the shaving process

Haircare

It's good to wash your hair every two to three days. This gives time for the hair's natural oils to provide moisture. Identify whether you have dry, oily, or normal hair so you can use the right products. If you have dandruff, use an anti-dandruff shampoo.

To avoid split ends, avoid excessive heat from hair dryers, curling irons, and straighteners. If you do want to use these heated styling tools, then it's a good idea to use heat-protective sprays or products. Trim split ends every three to six months and use hair sealants to reduce the chance of the split ends moving up the hair shaft!

Odor

Odor is created by sweat and hormones. Taking a shower or bathing twice a day will be beneficial. Washing in the morning clears away the nighttime sweat. An evening bath time ritual can serve to not only cleanse you from the day's sweat and grime but can also be a great way to prepare your mind to calm down in readiness for a good night's sleep.

Mouth

Brushing your teeth might seem like a no-brainer, but aside from just avoiding stinky breath, it's about the health of your entire body! If bacteria runs rampant in your mouth, then it can get into your bloodstream and impact your heart and body organs.

In the mouth, bacteria can cause gum disease and tooth decay (you can even lose your adult teeth!). It can also wear away at the enamel, leading to sensitive teeth.

You can minimize the risk of this happening by brushing your teeth twice a day and flossing once a day. Floss with inter-dental brushes, dental picks, dental floss, or pre-threaded floss. If you have braces, you may find that water flossing is a better alternative for you, as it uses a stream of water to help reach difficult places.

You can use your brush or a tongue scraper to gently brush over your tongue. This removes any plaque and bacteria that may have built up in a layer over your tongue and will help your breath smell fresh.

Armpits

Sweat is the body's way of cooling itself down. During hot weather, sweat can mix with hormones to create sweaty, smelly underarms! This smell is heightened during the pre-teen years when new hormones are still developing. You can counteract this by applying a deodorant or antiperspirant to your clean underarms before heading out for the day.

Some people sweat more than others. So, if your body is prone to excessive sweating that shows up as wet patches, you can wear loose clothing. This will encourage the excess sweat to remain on your body rather than seep into your clothes. Wearing dark colors can help reduce the appearance of wet stains near your underarms. Wearing a small, lightweight cotton T-shirt under your shirt can help absorb excess sweat before it appears as wet marks near the armpits of your external clothing.

Feet

Closed-toe shoes can result in stinky feet when you take off your shoes at the end of a hot day. This smell might be embarrassing. As before, bacteria is to blame for this smell as well. That means that dealing with the smell starts with washing and drying your feet well and airing out your shoes at the end of the day so they dry out, too. You can sprinkle foot powder inside your shoes or even use odor eaters (these are cool inserts that you can put in your shoes that eat up nasty smells!). This will help absorb excess moisture throughout the day. It will also serve to reduce the smell coming off your feet!

Groin

With the secretion of hormones and moisture, the vaginal area is also susceptible to the development of odors. Aside from washing and drying the vaginal area well during your daily bath time, you can also use intimate wipes to reduce the presence of sweat after exercise. During your monthly period, vaginal or intimate wipes can help make the process of changing absorbent material easier and cleaner.

When wiping yourself down with wipes, start in the vaginal area and then move toward your bottom. This way, you can avoid transferring bacteria from your bottom.

Stomach

Another area that can sweat excessively is the stomach area. Again, sweat attracts odors that have the potential to build up. You can use powders and special creams to absorb the moisture and odors in this area.

Alternative Way For All Body Parts to Stay Fresh

There are some products out there, like whole-body deodorants, meant specifically for all body parts, such as feet, bellies, pits, private areas, chests, and more. They are aluminum-free, pH-balanced, and free of things like parabens and harsh chemicals!

SELF CARE IDEAS

BUBBLE BATH

READ A BOOK

WATCH AN UPLIFTING MOVIE

FACE MASK NIGHT

MANI AND PEDI NIGHT

EAT AT YOUR FAVORITE RESTAURANT

SET SOME WEEKLY GOALS

TAKE A COZY NAP

JOURNAL

PLAY YOUR FAV VIDEO GAME

TREAT YOUR SELF TO SOMETHING

TRY A NEW ACTIVITY OR HOBBY

SELF CARE CHECKLIST

- [ ] _____
- [ ] _____
- [ ] _____
- [ ] _____
- [ ] _____
- [ ] _____

CHAPTER NINE

Mental Health Life Skills

Mindfulness Mastery & Conquering Your Emotions With Techniques I Bet You've Never Heard Of!

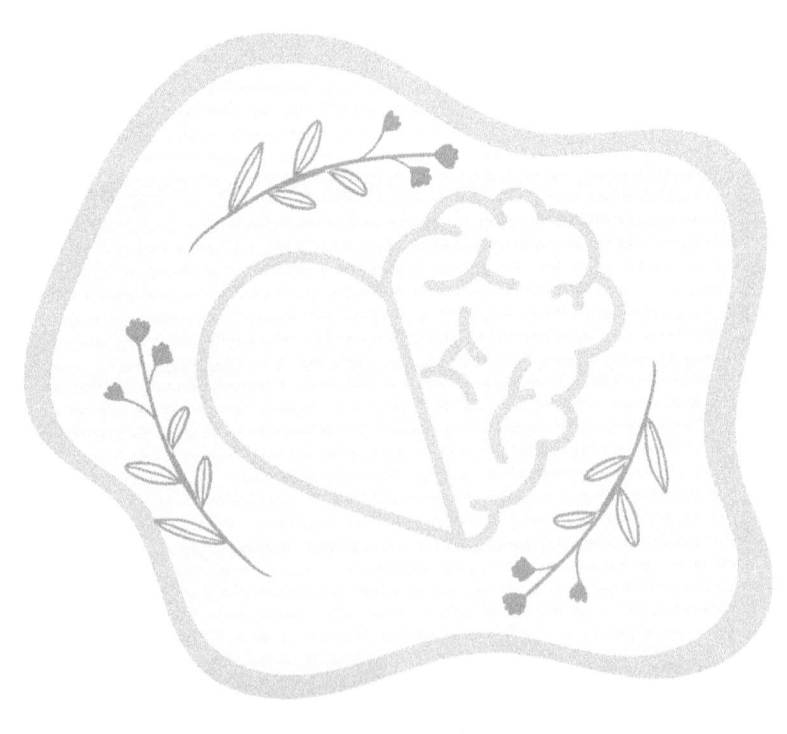

You live in a more demanding world than your parents did at your age. They did not have to worry about social media, keeping up with all of the rapidly changing technology, or being overwhelmed with the entire world's information at their fingertips! It seems that things were a little simpler back then, like hanging out with friends instead of keeping up with them online, sharing the family phone, only having a few TV channels, and getting their news from the paper.

In addition to a rapidly changing world, you are coping with hormonal changes. One of these hormones is cortisol, a hormone associated with increased bodily stress. It is no wonder that sometimes you feel overwhelmed. The question you might have right now is, "How can I deal with all of this and whatever other unknown factors may be introduced to me tomorrow? How can I maintain my composure and overcome life's daily challenges?"

Now, we are going to look at different ways to cope. The coping mechanisms you learn here will help you maintain your inner peace and balance so you can manage feelings of anxiety and tap into the wisdom you were born with!

Feeling Overwhelmed

With so many things happening all at once, it's easy to feel like you are losing control and not know what to concentrate on at any given time. At times like this, you may have the thought to just give up on everything altogether because it feels like no matter what you do, there is not enough time in the day to finish everything. My advice to you is that you don't need to quit! By all means, take a deep breath and get some rest. During that resting time, do more than just curl up in bed. Instead, do something that can reignite your mind and give you the ability to use a fresh approach to the tasks you need to complete!

Remember to treat yourself with kindness and self-love. These are activities that can help you wind down and reset your mind:

Self-Care Reset

A good way to deal with overwhelm is by giving yourself some grace and having some me time. Draw yourself a warm bubble bath. Fill it up with your favorite bubbles, bath bombs, and bath salts. Give yourself a full scrub down with a good exfoliator! While you're soaking, you can throw on a hair mask or treatment. You can also put on a rejuvenating face mask. When you get out of the bath, put on some on some smell-good lotion and throw on your favorite cozy pajamas or robe. Now it's time to take it easy, curl up in a blanket with some hot tea and watch your favorite move or read a book. Give yourself some grace because we all need a minute to recharge!

Moving Your Body

If you have too much excess energy to wind down in this way, it helps to move your body. This can involve taking a walk around the block. During the walk, you can pay attention to everything that you see around you. You can discuss the things you see with whomever you are walking with or write them down in your journal later. Engaging in sports also helps to get the blood flowing through your body. Find out what sports are available for you at your school or in your neighborhood. This can include sports such as squash, tennis, basketball, or dance.

Dance is a great way to enjoy music while mindfully moving your body. Joining dance classes can help you learn how to pay attention to the rhythm of a song while moving your body in unison. It is also a great way to make new friends.

Yoga and Stretching

Stretching your body by doing various yoga poses can help bring your thoughts into the present moment so your mind is not distracted by worries. Instead, you will be focused on moving and stretching your body. Here are a few yoga poses to get you started:

Child's Pose

Child's Pose

Kneel on the ground with your bottom resting on your feet or ankles. Drop your head forward so your forehead touches the ground while your arms are extended on either side of your thighs.

Mountain Pose

Mountain Pose

Stand with your feet together and your arms hanging on either side of your body. Breathe in and stretch your body upward as far as you can.

Warrior Pose

Warrior Pose

From the mountain pose, step forward with one foot while lowering your body so the knee is bent, and lift both arms above your head.

These are just a few beginner yoga poses to get you started, but I encourage you to learn more as your yoga journey progresses! Exercising will release endorphins that make you feel good while getting the blood flowing to your brain and the stress out of your body. If you get into the habit of engaging in physical exercise daily, it will help you to focus better throughout the day.

Tapping

Did you know that tapping on certain parts of the body can not only help calm you down but can reprogram subconscious beliefs that don't serve you into ones that do?! For example, you might subconsciously think, "I'm not good at geometry; I think I'm going to fail," but by tapping on the following points and saying positive affirmations, such as, "Even though I might find geometry challenging, I know that if I put my mind to it, I can master anything!" you will log the new, more empowering belief into your psyche!

By tapping on the following points, you can regulate your emotions and reprogram your subconscious mind! In my opinion, this is probably the most powerful way to train your brain for success, as it's free, extremely powerful, and can be done in a minute or two!

(Remember, most people use their dominant hand to tap, but it doesn't matter which hand you use!)

As you tap, make a statement about the matter you're having disempowering thoughts about, or that is causing you anxiety. You can also tap on positive things, like being grateful!

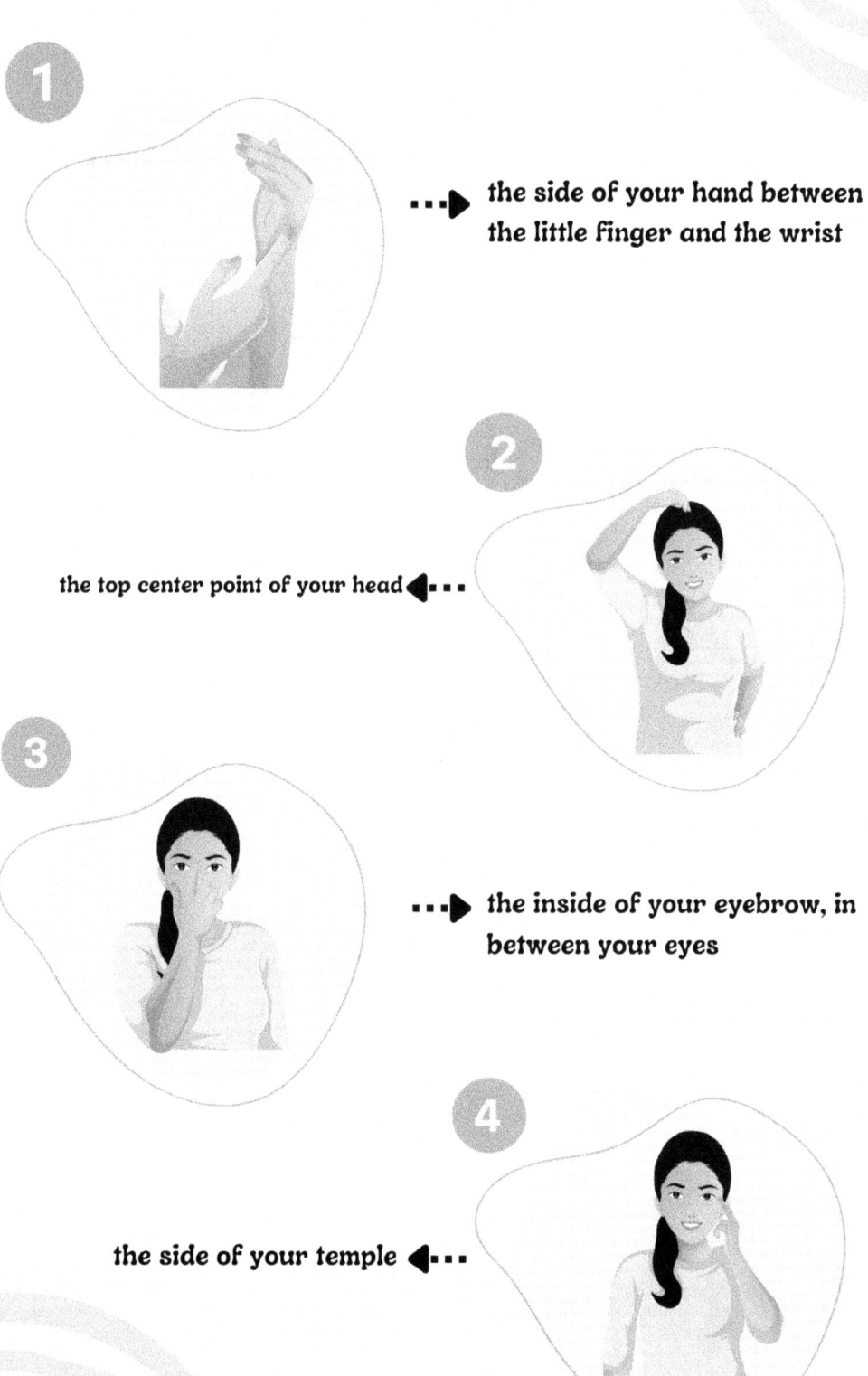

1. the side of your hand between the little finger and the wrist

2. the top center point of your head

3. the inside of your eyebrow, in between your eyes

4. the side of your temple

5 on the center of the bone below your eye

6 the center point above your mouth, just below your nose

7 the chin

8 below your collarbone

9 on the side of your ribcage below each armpit

Guided Tapping Exercise for Confidence

Tap along on the following areas, and say the following words out loud for a quick self-confidence booster! (Remember, you can tap on any subject, and you can find hundreds of amazing tapping videos online for free!)

Tapping on the side of your hand between the little finger and the wrist:

♥ "Even though I am really hard on myself and lack confidence, I choose to love, respect, and back myself."

♥ "Even though somewhere along the line, I got the idea that I wasn't good enough, I choose to love, respect, and back myself."

♥ "Even though I feel like the world is really competitive and overwhelming, I choose to love, respect, and back myself." (Now through the other tapping points)

Tapping on the top center point of your head:

♥ "All this lack of confidence in myself."

Tapping on the inside of your eyebrow, in between your eyes:

♥ "Somewhere along the line, I picked up the idea that I was less than other people."

Tapping on the side of your temple:

♥ "But I choose to question that idea now."

Tapping on the center of the bone below your eye:

♥ "Whether I picked up this idea from my family, friends, or somewhere else, I choose to see that I am just as important as anyone else."

Tapping on the center point above your mouth just below your nose:

♥ "And if anyone ever made me feel like I am not enough, then that is just a reflection of their own insecurity, and it has nothing to do with me."

Tapping on your chin:

♥ "So I'm choosing to feel really good about myself because I know I have so many incredible talents and a loving heart to share with the world."

Tapping below your collarbone:

♥ "And I choose to share my unique expression with the world and realize that I am a gift, not something to be ashamed of or hidden."

Tapping on the side of your ribcage below each armpit:

♥ "Knowing deep down that I have so much to offer the world, that I am so loved, and that I am a unique and an amazing expression of life!"

Tapping on the top center point of your head:

♥ "Knowing this through every cell of my body and all the way back through my life."

Now, take a deep breath!

The above exercise was just one round, but you can do as many rounds as you like for as long as you like (a round means going through all of the points 1 time). Remember, you can tap on any subject you like, like acing that chemistry exam, dealing with stage fright before playing a concert, or even getting over the fear of flying! The benefits you can get from tapping are endless!

Journaling

Writing things down is a good way to get ideas and feelings out of your head and onto paper. Once you have expressed your thoughts by writing them down, you will find that they are easier to process. Having your ideas expressed on paper also provides a good way to reflect on what happened in the past weeks or months and how it relates to current events. This can provide a learning opportunity, as it can help you discover things about yourself that you may not have been able to realize without writing them down. For example, you may begin to see patterns emerge. By reflecting on these patterns, you can begin to understand yourself and the beliefs that may be causing you to behave in certain ways. Often, these beliefs are subconscious or hidden from your everyday awareness. So, writing down your thoughts, reflections, and daily activities in your journal can help bring these to your awareness!

I personally struggled with journaling at first because I would get overwhelmed about what to write. I would get too caught up in my head and couldn't even get a word down! What helped me is realizing that your words don't have to make sense or have perfect punctuation; they can just consist of the random thoughts that come into your head that second! And from there, it will just start flowing. You can write about your goals, your feelings, and your emotions, draw pictures, or you could even do writing prompts. Here, I've put some below to get you started!

Daily Journal

Things that weren't so positive?

The postive things that happened:

How can I turn these negatives into a better tomorrow?

Overall mood

What am I grateful for?

Social Media

When you use your social media accounts, keep in mind that whatever people post online is not a true reflection of their lives. Each popular photo and video is carefully thought of to get the most likes. Keep this in mind when you go online so you don't compare yourself to others. You never know what is really going on in the person's life whose post you're looking at; you're only seeing what they WANT you to see. You have to remember that we live in a world where every picture and video can easily be edited via software and filters, which creates a false sense of what we should look like or how successful we should be. You also don't know how much time was wasted with numerous attempts to create the perfect post.

When you post statements, respond to posts, and upload pictures and videos, remember that what you post could reach lots of people and last a long time. So, if you are not certain about how other people will perceive what you are saying, do not post it. Instead, really think about what you're posting before you click that "post" button. We all have moments where sadness and anger get the best of us, but this is not a good time to post; don't let the adrenaline post for you. You don't want to be in a situation in the future where you regret something you posted online. Once you have uploaded something, even deleting it may not remove it completely, as somebody may take a screenshot of what you have written within the 30 seconds that it takes to change your mind and press delete. Where social media is concerned, it is better to err on the side of caution.

Another way to protect your mental health when it comes to social media is by establishing boundaries around your online persona. Limit your profile so only trusted people can engage with your posts and interact freely with you. If somebody says something that makes you uncomfortable in any way, you can block them and restrict them from your profile. They do not have the right to invade your personal online space, and they definitely should not be given access to impacting your positive state of mind!

Remember to limit your time online, as overindulging in social media can take up too much of your precious time. How many times do you catch yourself doom-scrolling? All those countless hours spent looking at other people's lives can be better spent on yourself and achieving your own goals! With this in mind, it may be a good idea to set a timer when you go on social media. You can use your phone's alarm to do this or find an app that helps you limit your online activity.

Practicing Mindfulness

You don't always have the opportunity to take time off to pamper yourself and watch a movie to help ease your mind. At times like these, you need to find other means to stop anxiety from building within you. One way to do this is to practice mindfulness. What this means is to pay attention to the thoughts and emotions you are having without acting on them. You simply observe them. The fancy word for being consciously aware of your thoughts is metacognition!

Take a moment to pay attention to the feelings that come up within you. Perhaps you feel sadness in your belly or a tight anger in your chest and throat? Practice feeling where they appear in your body but not acting on them. The moment you act on your emotions is the moment that they are controlling you! The goal is to do the opposite and show them that you are in charge of your reactions!

Life is 10% what happens to you and 90% how you react. –Charles Swindoll

Mindfulness Exercise

Whenever you feel as though your emotions are running out of control or your thoughts are spiraling, there is one thing you must do. Stop. Stop what you are doing and pay attention to your feelings. Pay attention to your thoughts. Ask yourself where the thoughts are coming from. Ask yourself what the source of the emotions is.

Try this exercise whenever you are feeling overwhelmed by emotion or you simply just want to grow your mindfulness skills:

♥ Stop right in the tracks of your emotion or painful thought.

♥ Identify where in your body this sensation is appearing. Can you feel fear or sadness in your stomach? Anger clenching in your throat?

♥ Do not react to the emotion, and do not let your mind get pulled into a train of thought.

♥ Simply observe the emotion as a sensation in your body. Do not label it as either bad or good.

♥ Imagine the emotion as a cube of ice and imagine dropping it into a glass of hot water.

♥ Imagine the warm water melting the cube away bit by bit, just like your awareness is melting away the emotion in your body.

♥ Stay in this observation until the ice cube that represents your emotion is melted away completely. (It will pass, I promise!)

This observation and melting away of your emotions via mindful attention is called "the fire of yoga" by some people!

The more you practice this mindful exercise, the more your mindful power will grow, and you will be able to deal with stressful situations like a boss while others around you may crumble! Everyone will be blown away by your calmness and will want to know what your secret is!

Mindful Activities

You can also do some mindful activities to take your mind off whatever is bothering you. By focusing on something else, you can regulate your mind and emotions. Doing these activities with friends and family makes them more enjoyable and provides you with opportunities to strengthen your relationships. Some activities you could try include:

♥ Being creative: Color in a picture, draw, play an instrument, or even help paint a wall if your parents or guardians are doing some renovating.

♥ Listening to your favorite music: Do this with your eyes closed so you can appreciate the music fully and shut off external stimuli. The music will uplift your soul. Hear how the different instruments blend together. Imagine that you were a professional dancer; how would you choreograph a dance to the song you are listening to? If this activity inspires you to move your body in dance and you have the space to do it, get up and dance. It is a continuation of enjoying the music.

♥ Enjoying a cup of tea: Use all your senses to enjoy the tea. Smell it, taste it, and feel the temperature and the sensation of the tea swirling in your mouth and going down your throat.

♥ Making a list of things you are grateful for: This is called a gratitude list. Try and have different things to put on the list every day. Knowing that you will be writing at least one thing in your gratitude list at the end of the day can make you more aware of the positive experiences you have.

♥ Spending time with your pets: Play with them, feed them, and observe their antics. This can be very calming. Observing animals can teach you how to live life without judgment. If you do not have any pets, ask your parents or guardians if you can go to the zoo. Spend time watching the animals there and learn from their behavior.

♥ Meditating: Close your eyes and focus on your breathing, listen to the sounds around you, and focus on a single thought. This will calm your mind down so it is less aroused and less prone to anxiety.

♥ Walking in nature: Taking a walk in nature is incredibly rejuvenating for your body, mind, and spirit, and it will fill you with a sense of calm. Hearing the wind flowing through the leaves of tall trees and listening to the sounds of birds singing is my favorite thing in the world!

Any enjoyable activity that calms you down and helps you focus your attention on something enjoyable can be adopted as a mindful activity.

Girl, you got this! Remember that when you continually use these practices, you will have more control when the world feels heavy. You can get through anything because you are smart, strong, powerful, and resilient!

BREATHING TECHNIQUE

1   Breathe in for four seconds.

2   Hold for two seconds.

3   Exhale for four seconds.

4   Hold for two seconds.

5   Repeat four times.

CHAPTER TEN

Safety Life Skills

**How to Arm Yourself with Confidence
and Street Smarts, Online and In Person!**

In this chapter, we're going to look at all the ways that we can stay safe in the world, both online and in person. Why is this important? Well, because, unfortunately, there are some people out there with some bad intentions that are best avoided at all costs! These could be at the mall, in the street, or even on an online social media site. So, eyes up, pay attention, and check out these safety tips that could save you and your friends one day!

Staying Safe In the World

♥ Memorize the phone numbers of family members and close friends. This way, you will always know which numbers to reach out to for help if you lose your phone and need to use a public phone.

♥ Also, memorize your home address and the addresses of family and friends. In an emergency, you can give this information to emergency personnel, who can then help you get to safety. If you visit family or friends in another town, make sure that you know how to provide an address if you get lost. Also, memorize the phone numbers of where you are staying.

♥ If you have to walk somewhere, go with friends. Avoid walking in isolated places. Try to always stay where there are people around.

♥ There is safety in numbers. Walking alone makes it easier for dubious strangers to approach you. If something happens when you are in a group, others can alert the authorities.

♥ If you are walking alone, try not to wear headphones or listen to loud music. This can stop you from hearing people calling you or warning you of danger. It also allows you to hear sirens, oncoming traffic, and anything else you need to be aware of. When you are in public places, you can turn vigilance into a game. Pretend you are a private investigator who needs to report what is happening in an area. This will help you avoid being so focused on your phone that you miss important events taking place around you.

♥ Avoid talking to strangers. One of their tricks could be trying to make it appear as if they know you so that others around you may be confused about whether you are in danger or not.

♥ When you are out in public, pay attention to your environment. This includes knowing where security officers are and identifying exits, restrooms, police officers, and any staff who may be around. Knowing where police officers, security, and staff are will make it easier for you to identify who to go to should you need help.

♥ Take your eyes off your cell phone while you are in public. Looking at the screen makes you less aware of what is happening in the world around you. You could end up tripping over items that are lying on the ground or bumping into stationary objects! When you are too busy looking at your phone, a stranger could come and steal your bag, and you would not even notice that it was gone until it was too late. Keeping your phone out of sight gives you the ability to be more vigilant in your observations about what is taking place around you.

♥ When you go out with friends, be honest with your parents or guardians and tell them where you are going and who you will be with. Switch on the location setting on your cell phone and share your location with your parents or guardians. However, do not share your location with anybody else, whether it is a close friend or on social media. The wrong people could get access to the information. Even if you are enjoying yourself wherever you are, you do not need to immediately share your location and pictures on social media and with your friends. Wait until you have left an area before you post on social media where you were and what you did that day. Keeping your location private keeps you safe from strangers and stalkers!

♥ Remember to always leave the house with a fully charged phone so your phone can continue to alert your parents or guardians of your location, even if you are unable to talk to them at a given time. Make sure to keep a charger with you and, even better, a power bank as well!

♥ If you are somewhere with a group of friends or with your relatives, do not separate yourself from the group. Ask somebody to accompany you to the toilet so you do not become isolated. You could even go to the restroom in a group to ensure that all members of the group are safe and accounted for at all times. This will stop anybody from getting lost.

♥ Should you need to use public transport to travel anywhere, plan for each step of your journey. Know where you are going, what stops will be made, and who will meet you at each step of the way. Travel during the daytime when it is easier to identify what is happening around you. If something goes wrong or if you are delayed during a morning trip, there will still be daylight hours left to continue the trip and arrive safely.

In Person Safety
key points

Memorize Your Family's Phone Numbers & Addresses!

Keep Your Eyes Up & Off Your Phone. Always Be Aware Of Your Surroundings!

Avoid Going Anywhere Alone; There Is Safety In Numbers!

Try To Avoid Using Headphones While Alone In Public. Or, At Minimum, Take One Earbud out & Turn It Low!

Always Locate Emergency Exits, Emergency Personal, Staff, & Phones While Out In Public!

Online Safety

While the internet is a great way of staying connected, like in the physical world, we need to be aware that sketchy people also exist online. This means that we need to be safe online as well!

♥ Make sure that your device is safe. Having a safe device starts with always keeping your operating system up to date. This reduces the system vulnerabilities that hackers can use to access your devices. Software patches and updates to the operating system are often created to close off any system vulnerabilities that hackers have learned to exploit.

♥ If your operating system is up to date, the next point of weakness could be your password. If your passwords are easy to guess, then anybody who wants access to your email, schedule, or social media could connect remotely to access your personal information. Passwords that are easy to guess include your pet's name, your first school, your mother's maiden name, or your date of birth. Instead, use a word that is not easy for people to guess. Add a special character and a few numbers so it is not easy to crack your password.

♥ Having a brilliant password will not protect your information if you are freely handing your password out for others to see. This is what happens when we enter our passwords onto our devices while using unsecured public Wi-Fi. Some hackers will even set up free Wi-Fi with the intention of stealing your information. They set up their free Wi-Fi in such a way that they can see all information that passes through their network. This data can include your personal information and passwords. So, avoid using unsecured public Wi-Fi. If you desperately need to use these networks, do not use them for sites that require you to log in. Also, avoid sharing personal information while using these networks.

♥ Another trick that hackers use is online scams. One way they do this is by sending official-looking emails. You can always tell from the email address whether an email is from a real source or not. The domain of the email address should align with the website that you know. If the domain ends differently from the website or is from a different domain, it is not likely to be genuine. Do not click links in emails unless you are 100% sure of the origins of the email. These links can open websites that look like official sites. When you enter information into these fake sites, your information will be captured for use in accessing the real site. For example, you could receive an email telling you that some details at your bank are out of date and your account will be closed soon if you do not change your details. A link will be provided so you can click on it and change your details. If you click on that link, a website may open that looks exactly like your bank's site. On this site, you will attempt to log in with your real login details and fail. The scammers will capture these details and use them to access your real bank account so they can transfer your money out of your account. Scary!

♥ If you get an email you are not sure about, talk to your parents and/or guardians about it first. Also, be on the lookout for any fake emergency in the email! If you doubt that an email is real, you can show it to your parents or guardians so they can help determine if it's legit or not. Sometimes, spelling mistakes and incorrect logos will give a scam away!

♥ Avoid opening any attachments in emails from unknown addresses. These could be gifs, PDFs, dangerous executables (exe), or any other format. Sometimes, these attachments have computer worms and viruses embedded in them. By opening these documents, you could be activating a virus that can infiltrate your computer and send your personal information to its creator!

♥ Recognize that scammers can also send these messages via text message. So, do not click on links that you receive via text message if you are not sure of their origin. These could be directing you to a site that steals your personal information or makes your mobile device vulnerable to attackers!

♥ Some of the fun interactive games on social media that give answers based on the responses you provide are just a cover. The real purpose of these games is often to collect enough information so that they can guess your passwords and hack into your social media and email accounts. When you engage with these pages and sites, you might as well disable your password or just email your username and password to the hackers!

♥ So, aside from not sharing your personal information on scammer pages and sites, also avoid sharing too much personal information on your social media accounts. When you post pictures or videos of events, do it after the event has passed and you are safely home. Also, avoid sharing your current location. Instead, share the location of your fun outing after you have had your fun and left.

♥ It can be really exciting to share photos on social media when you're on vacation or at your favorite mall. However, for your safety, you should post them AFTER you have left that premise. That way, you're not sharing your location with anyone that doesn't need that information.

♥ When posting online, turn your geotag off to avoid the same.

♥ Friend requests can get confusing sometimes. A new friend requester might have several friends in common with you, but you might not personally know them or even recognize them. DO NOT assume that your friends personally know them just because they added them. Just avoid adding anyone you don't know, PERIOD!

Now that you have secured your environment and are aware of the potential pitfalls, go on and have some fun. Just always remember that you've got to be safe!

Online Safety

key points

Open Your Emails Wisely. Be Wary Of Links & Attachments.

Wait Until After You Have Left A Recognizable Location Before Posting On Social Media.

Don't Tag Your Location On Social Media.

Don't Add Anyone On Social Media You Don't Know.

Keep Your Phone/ Computer Up To Date To Avoid Viruses, & Make Your Passwords Strong.

CHAPTER ELEVEN

Syncing Your Cycle Life Skills

Understanding Your Period, Ovulatory Cycle Routines, & How to Take Advantage of All 4 Phases!

Hey, bestie, it's time to be vulnerable and talk about the changes that you're going through or will eventually experience. You're going through the biological switch from a girl to a woman. Maybe your friends have already talked to you about it, or maybe you're currently experiencing it, but what I'm talking about is your period. In this chapter, we'll go over what it is, what you might be feeling, when it could happen, being prepared, and a really cool way to not just track it but sync it and create routines around each phase that not even most adults know about! The average age to start having your period is between the ages of 10 and 15. It usually happens around once every month. Maybe you've been embarrassed or shy to talk about it or ask questions, but don't worry! I'm here to give you the basics.

Build Up to Menstruation

As you know by now, hormones are very active in the body. Like other processes we have looked at, the menstruation process starts with hormones. In this case, hormones called progesterone and estrogen are released from your ovaries (more about ovaries in a minute). These hormones make the uterus lining build up. Now, the lining of your uterus is ready for an egg to attach. When there's not a fertilized egg, the lining of your uterus sheds and bleeds. This is known as a period.

What Are Ovaries?

Ovaries are the parts of your body you're born that hold eggs, also called ovums. The ovaries have millions of little eggs and release one every month!

Being Prepared

Sanitary Protection

Be prepared by having sanitary towels, or pads, on hand to absorb the blood that flows out. You can stick the pads onto the part of your underwear that directly faces your vagina. Period underwear is an alternative reusable option that incorporates the pad into the underwear. The absorbent material from the pad will retain the blood that flows out. In this way, you will avoid staining your clothes or bedsheets with blood from your period. You can change your sanitary pad every three to four hours to ensure that it remains absorbent enough to avoid any blood overflowing.

Other than sanitary pads, you can also use tampons, menstrual cycle cups, or menstrual disks to help you manage the blood flow. Unlike pads that stick to the underwear, these need to be inserted into the vaginal opening. In this way, they can catch the blood before it lands on the underwear. If you want to find out more about these methods, ask your parents and/or guardians to give you the information.

Make sure to have a sanitary pad and know about all of the methods beforehand so you'll be prepared when it happens!

Clues From Your Body

By the time you start your period, several changes will have already taken place in your body, making it look different over time. Once your body starts producing estrogen, it causes fat tissue in your breasts to grow. The result of this is that you will start to have breasts. When ovulation has occurred (when your eggs get released), your breasts might start to feel tender or slightly bigger. This is one of the symptoms that may indicate to you that your period is on the way. However, that is just one step in the menstrual cycle.

The menstrual cycle is a 28-day cycle. The first day of your period is considered to be day one. At each stage along the cycle, your body reacts differently as the level of different hormones secreted into your body varies. Try to pay attention to the changes that take place in your body throughout the month. Knowing how to cope with the impact of these changes will help you live a less stressful life!

Premenstrual Syndrome (PMS)

With all the hormones and physical changes that take place in your body over a short space of time, it can become overwhelming. The body will be flooded with hormones. Progesterone and estrogen are both high in the days after ovulation and before your period. The hormones cause emotional and physical stress in the body that results in a variety of symptoms that are called PMS symptoms. These can include tender breasts, irritability, frustration, depression, fatigue, and cravings for different foods. People may not understand why you are so "moody." Unless you are tracking your menstrual cycle, you may not understand the reason why everything does not seem to be going your way.

Luckily, you can manage the symptoms that accompany the hormone-induced mood swings. By understanding that your menstrual cycle goes through different phases, you can align your lifestyle with each phase. Done properly, this will help you manage the impact of the hormonal changes that are experienced at different times of the month. The method that is used to do this is called cycle syncing. You are lucky to have access to this tool, as many adult women are not aware of its existence yet!

Syncing Your Cycles

Alisa Vitti, who created the MyFlo app, devised a concept called cycle syncing. This involves adjusting your lifestyle throughout the month so it aligns with your menstrual cycle. There are four stages of the menstrual cycle. At each stage, you can incorporate minor shifts that will help you cope with the changes at each stage. These shifts help counteract the effect that changing hormones have on your behavior, emotions, energy levels, moods, craving for different types of food, and need for different types of exercise. Knowing what to incorporate into your lifestyle at each stage can help to reduce the strain on your body, emotions, and psychological well-being!

Menstrual Phase

♥ Consider the first day of your period to be day one of your cycle. The menstrual phase of your cycle occurs from day one to day five. The hormones progesterone and estrogen are low at this time. This results in the shedding of the lining of the womb, which is what causes your period to appear.

♥ At this time, reduce the amount of salt in your diet. Replace fatty foods with foods that are high in omega-3 fatty acids. This can include salmon, tree nuts, and flaxseed. Omega-3s will help reduce menstrual cramps.

♥ Consume foods with a high iron content to cater for the iron lost during menstrual bleeding. These foods include lean red meat, leafy greens, and legumes, such as lentils. To help improve the rate at which iron is absorbed into your body, consume foods high in vitamin C, such as red peppers, broccoli, and citrus fruit.

♥ Drink soothing drinks, like herbal teas. Chamomile is a good option for calming you down.

♥ Your energy levels are low at this time due to estrogen levels being at their lowest point in the cycle. So, instead of strenuous exercise, you should rest during this phase. If you feel the need to do some sort of workout, concentrate on calming exercises, such as basic yoga, stretching, Pilates, and walking.

Period Tracker

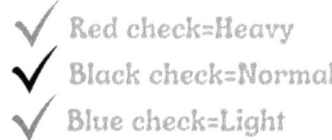

Red check=Heavy
Black check=Normal
Blue check=Light

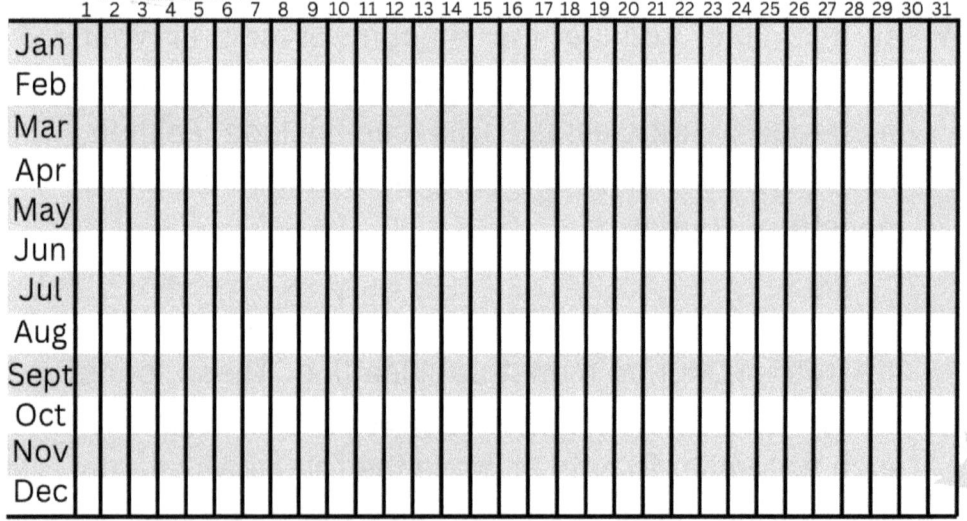

	1	2	3	4	5	6	7	8	9	10	11	12	13	14	15	16	17	18	19	20	21	22	23	24	25	26	27	28	29	30	31
Jan																															
Feb																															
Mar																															
Apr																															
May																															
Jun																															
Jul																															
Aug																															
Sept																															
Oct																															
Nov																															
Dec																															

Daily Routine for the Menstrual Phase

Morning: Do some easy stretching exercises before you get ready for school. Sit on the floor with your legs spread in a V shape. Try to touch your toes and hold for 5 to 10 seconds.

Daytime: Take a walk outside with a friend or a sibling. Enjoy the daytime light, and remember to take deep breaths as you walk. Include warming, cozy foods like stew or soup. The warm foods will relieve cramps. Include red meat or pulses, such as lentils, in your meals. This will help to replace the blood that is lost through menstruation.

Night: Drink a cup of chamomile tea while reading your favorite book before bed. Take some time to reflect on the day and write in your journal!

Follicular Phase

♥ The follicular phase occurs between day 6 and day 14 of your cycle. Progesterone and estrogen production start rising, and this is about the time your period ends.

♥ At this stage, you will start to feel creative and energetic! So, it's a good time to engage in creative activities such as baking, drawing, or decorating!

♥ Eating pumpkin seeds, flaxseeds, and avocados

will introduce healthy fats into your diet during the follicular phase. Leafy green vegetables and steamed vegetables will help balance your estrogen levels. Steamed vegetables include cauliflower, broccoli, and cabbage. Consuming fermented food during this stage will help produce more happy hormones, such as serotonin, in your brain. This will contribute to your creativity. Fermented foods you can consume include yogurt, sauerkraut, pickles, and kombucha!

♥ Exercises to get the most benefit from this time would be cardio, pilates, hiking, or cycling.

Daily Routine for the Follicular Phase

Morning: Start the morning with some resistance training. You can do some squats or some wall Pilates to get your day started!

Daytime: Set up a game of tennis for after school with your favorite opponent. This will give you time to work out and get in a nice social chat afterward!

Night: You can take time to do some brainstorming for new projects. Put as much detail into planning as you can while you have the follicular phase energy that helps you be creative at this time of the month!

Ovulation Phase

♥ The ovulation phase takes place from day 15 to day

17. This is when your estrogen levels are at their highest. The hormone progesterone continues to rise. Testosterone levels also start to rise at this time.

♥ Eat a lot of fruit, vegetables, and nuts. Focus on flushing toxins and excess estrogen out of your system by drinking a lot of water. Eat lots of cruciferous vegetables. This will help you continue the balancing of your estrogen levels.

♥ During this phase, energy levels are high due to high levels of estrogen, progesterone, and testosterone that are flooding your body. High-intensity aerobic workouts, such as kickboxing, spinning, and a high-impact hit class, will take advantage of the energy rush that you are experiencing at a time when you feel like you are working out at your best!

Daily Routine for the Ovulation Phase

Morning: Have a healthy breakfast of fresh fruit or oatmeal. Drink lots of water, and remember to pack water for the day. During this time, your body will need to flush out excess estrogen.

Daytime: Try to exhaust yourself with a high-intensity workout. This can include a kickboxing class, a sprint on the field, or a spinning class.

Night: If you have a project to work on, this is the time to implement as much of it as possible. Use the excess energy to finish any project that may have had a slow start. If you have a social media account, take some time to record a few videos and schedule them for later on in the cycle when you will not have as much energy to work on your social media posts. This could be a good time to check off all the things on your to-do list that you've been ignoring!

Luteal Phase

♥ The luteal phase happens on day 18 and continues until day 28. At this time, both estrogen and progesterone are high.

♥ As hormonal levels increase at the beginning of this phase and then decrease toward the end, it is important to balance the extreme hormonal changes that your body goes through. You can do this by eating food that makes your body feel good despite the hormonal levels it is experiencing. Eating foods such as dark chocolate, pumpkin seeds, and leafy green vegetables will help produce serotonin in your body. This is due to the magnesium in these foods. The iron content of these foods will also help boost your body in preparation for the loss of blood that will take place in the menstrual phase. You can further reduce the strain on your body by avoiding red meat, salt, and dairy during this phase.

♥ The luteal phase is a good time to engage in muscle-building exercises, such as weight lifting and Pilates.

Daily Routine for the Luteal Phase

Morning: Start your day with some stretching exercises.

Daytime: Take an afternoon walk around the block or do some yoga. Have a restful afternoon without too many activities planned for the day.

Night: Have a quiet night with a book and a face mask. Do some self-pampering activities, like painting your toenails!

Customize Your Chart

These are all guidelines and can be used to start your journey of being mindful about what you eat and how you exercise throughout your cycle! Take into account that you are a unique individual. So, you may or may not be able to eat certain foods, you may not be used to certain exercises, and you may not have some of these things accessible to you, but there are so many ways to customize your own unique chart just for you! So, be aware of how your body responds to these adjustments. You may find that the number of days that your body remains in each stage of the cycle differs from what is written here. Make your own chart, starting with day one of your period, and continue to monitor how you feel. Also, realize that not all cycles are exactly 28 days. Your chart needs to take this into account so you can benefit from implementing the cycle sync method!

To get you started on customizing your own chart, the first example shows what to write in each section. Then, you can fill out the blank version.

CYCLE SYNCING

MENSTRUATION PHASE

DURATION: Fill in how long your Menstruation phase typically lasts!

MOVEMENT: Fill in your favorite types of exercise that correlate with the Menstruation phase!

ACTIVITIES: Fill in your favorite activities that correlate with the Menstruation phase!

FOOD: Fill in foods you enjoy here that correlate with the Menstruation Phase!

FOLLICULAR PHASE

DURATION: Fill in how long your Follicular phase typically lasts!

MOVEMENT: Fill in your favorite types of exercise that correlate with the Follicular phase!

ACTIVITIES: Fill in your favorite activities that correlate with the Follicular phase!

FOOD: Fill in foods you enjoy here that correlate with the Follicular Phase!

LUTEAL PHASE

DURATION: Fill in how long your Luteal phase typically lasts!

MOVEMENT: Fill in your favorite types of exercise that correlate with the Luteal phase!

ACTIVITIES: Fill in your favorite activities that correlate with the Luteal phase!

FOOD: Fill in foods you enjoy here that correlate with the Luteal Phase!

OVULATION PHASE

DURATION: Fill in how long your Ovulation phase typically lasts!

MOVEMENT: Fill in your favorite types of exercise that correlate with the Ovulation phase!

ACTIVITIES: Fill in your favorite activities that correlate with the Ovulation phase!

FOOD: Fill in foods you enjoy here that correlate with the Ovulation Phase!

CYCLE SYNCING

MENSTRUATION PHASE

DURATION:

MOVEMENT:

ACTIVITIES:

FOOD:

FOLLICULAR PHASE

DURATION:

MOVEMENT:

ACTIVITIES:

FOOD:

LUTEAL PHASE

DURATION:

MOVEMENT:

ACTIVITIES:

FOOD:

OVULATION PHASE

DURATION:

MOVEMENT:

ACTIVITIES:

FOOD:

CONCLUSION

You Grow Girl! This Is Your Moment, Now Own It!

Congratulations on reaching the end of this book! It is so information-packed that you probably want to reflect and implement everything. My advice is to take your time and refer to it often, especially because each chapter addresses a different aspect of your journey.

As you encounter different situations at home, socially, and with your body, this book will be a trusted companion to guide you through your tweens. You can step out in confidence, knowing that you have the knowledge you need to address most of the challenges that life will throw at you. Now go and get your glow up—the world is waiting for you!

References

Anderson, K. (2011). Discussing menstruation with your daughter: What's a period? Children's Hospital Los Angeles. https://www.chla.org/blog/advice-experts/discussing-menstruation-your-daughter-whats-period

Are you being bullied? How to deal with bullies. (n.d). STOMP Out Bullying. https://www.stompoutbullying.org/how-to-deal-with-bullies

Ayeni-Bepo, A. (n.d). Teach your child how to deal with school gossip and rumors. Overcome With Us. https://overcomewithus.com/children/teach-your-child-how-to-deal-with-school-gossip-and-rumors

Becker, S. (2023). ETFs vs. Mutual funds: how to choose the right investment. Time. https://time.com/personal-finance/article/etfs-vs-mutual-funds

Beresin, G. (n.d). 11 self-care tips for teens and young adults. The MGH Clay Center for Young Healthy Minds. https://www.mghclaycenter.org/parenting-concerns/11-self-care-tips-for-teens-and-young-adults

Bottaro, A. (2023). What is a nodule? Very Well Health. https://www.verywellhealth.com/nodule-7106246

Brennan, D., Turley, R., Wojcik, S. (n.d). Exercise and teenagers. Health Encyclopedia. https://www.urmc.rochester.edu/encyclopedia/content.aspx?ContentTypeID=90&ContentID=P01602

Capecchi, S . (2022). Mindfulness for teens: How it works, benefits, & 11 exercises to try. Choosing Therapy. https://www.choosingtherapy.com/mindfulness-for-teens

Cherney, K . (2019). 11 ways to keep your teeth healthy. Healthline. https://www.healthline.com/health/dental-and-oral-health/best-practices-for-healthy-teeth

Desai, R . (2021). How to build the best teenage skin care routine. Apotheco Pharmacy Group. https://www.apothecopharmacy.com/blog/how-to-build-the-best-teenage-skin-care-routine

Dr. Thais Aliabadi Education Team. (2021). FDA names potentially bad ingredients in sunscreen: what you need to know: What you need to know. Dr. Thais Aliabadi Education Team. https://www.draliabadi.com/womens-health-blog/potentially-bad-ingredients-in-sunscreen/

Faryadian, S., Khosravi, A . (2015). Effects of prenatal exposure to different colors on offspring's mood. Iran J Basic Med Sci. https://www.ncbi.nlm.nih.gov/pmc/articles/PMC4764109

Gavin, ML. (n.d). 5 ideas for better sleep. KidsHealth. https://kidshealth.org/en/teens/tips-sleep.html

Gupta, S . (2022). The impact of self-respect on your life. Verywell Mind. https://www.verywellmind.com/self-respect-importance-influences-and-strategies-for-improvement-6823525

Hate flossing? 5 flossing alternatives. (2018). The Center for Cosmetic & Family Dentistry. https://www.destindentist.com/hate-flossing-5-flossing-alternatives

Higuera, V., Raypole, C . (2023). PMS: premenstrual syndrome symptoms, treatments, and more. Healthline. https://www.healthline.com/health/premenstrual-syndrome

Healthy eating during adolescence. (n.d). Hopkins Medicine. https://www.hopkinsmedicine.org/health/wellness-and-prevention/healthy-eating-during-adolescence

How to do decorations with Blu Tack. (n.d). Bostik. https://diy.bostik.com/en-MY/how-to/how-to-do-decorations-blu-tack

How to use a fire extinguisher. (2023). WikiHow. https://www.wikihow.com/Use-a-Fire-Extinguisher

How to use Command strips for hanging pictures. (n.d). 3M. https://www.command.com/3M/en_US/command/how-to-use/picture-hanging-strips

Hudson, A . (2022). 13 ways on how to help your teen make friends. Ashley Hudson Therapy. https://www.ashleyhudsontherapy.com/post/13-ways-on-how-to-help-your-teen-make-friends

Hydration tips for children. (2022). Health Direct. https://www.healthdirect.gov.au/hydration-tips-for-children

Kahn, A . (2023). What causes pustules?. Healthline. https://www.healthline.com/health/pustules

Krupp, A . (2023). Cycle syncing: Matching your health style to your menstrual cycle. Healthline. https://www.healthline.com/health/womens-health/guide-to-cycle-syncing-how-to-start

Lake, R. (2023). Best ways to send money as a teen. Investopedia. https://www.investopedia.com/best-ways-to-send-money-as-a-teen-7152565

Mandal, A . (n.d). Acne causes. News Medical Life Sciences. https://www.news-medical.net/health/Acne-Causes.aspx

Mandal, A. (n.d). What is acne? News Medical Life Sciences. https://www.news-medical.net/health/Acne.aspx

McCracken, A. (2022). How to love yourself for real, according to therapists. SELF. https://www.self.com/story/how-to-love-yourself

Myers, I. (2022). EWG's dirty dozen guide to food chemicals: the top 12 to avoid. EWG. https://www.ewg.org/consumer-guides/ewgs-dirty-dozen-guide-food-chemicals-top-12-avoid

Nawale, P.B. (2022). 16 effective skin care tips for teenagers. Skinkraft. https://skinkraft.com/blogs/articles/skin-care-tips-for-teenagers

Newman, T. (2023). What to know about cysts. Medical News Today. https://www.medicalnewstoday.com/articles/160821

Nutrition and exercise throughout your menstrual cycle. (2023). Women's Health. https://health.clevelandclinic.org/nutrition-and-exercise-throughout-your-menstrual-cycle

Oral health: a window to your overall health. (2021). Mayo Clinic. https://www.mayoclinic.org/healthy-lifestyle/adult-health/in-depth/dental/art-20047475

Pacheco, D. (2023). Best temperature for sleep. Sleep Foundation. https://www.sleepfoundation.org/bedroom-environment/best-temperature-for-sleepv

Palmer, A. (2023). Acne papules causes and treatments. Very Well Health. https://www.verywellhealth.com/papule-definition-of-an-acne-papule-15541

Pantazi, C., Krause, A. (2021). There's a secret expiration date on your makeup that you probably didn't know existed. Insider. https://www.insider.com/how-to-tell-if-makeup-is-expired-symbol-2017-4?amp

Royal, J. (2023). 11 best investment apps in October 2023. Bankrate. https://www.bankrate.com/investing/best-investment-apps

Scott, S. (2023). 17 mindfulness activities and exercises for teens in 2023. Happier Human. https://www.happierhuman.com/mindfulness-activities-teenagers

Sloww. (2018). Konmari method: 5-step decluttering cheat sheet. Medium. https://medium.com/@slowwco/konmari-method-5-step-decluttering-cheat-sheet-a1d1cc873e17

Smith, N. (n.d). Which colour is right for me? Dopamine Décor. https://dopaminedecor.com/colour-psychology

Society Insurance Team. (2018). How to use a fire extinguisher: an easy 4-step process. Society Insurance . https://societyinsurance.com/blog/how-to-use-a-fire-extinguisher-an-easy-4-step-process

Solis-Moreira, J. (n.d). 6 ways to practice self-love. Forbes. https://www.forbes.com/health/mind/how-to-practice-self-love/

Sophia, W. (2013). The difference between egoism and self-love. Exploring Deeper. https://www.exploringdeeper.com/the-difference-between-egoism-and-self-love

Stalter, K. (n.d). Investing for teens: How to invest money as a teenager. USNews Money. https://money.usnews.com/investing/articles/investing-for-teens-how-to-invest-money-as-a-teenager

Sunscreen SPF and skin protection. (2023). W.S. Badger Company. https://www.badgerbalm.com/pages/what-is-spf-sunscreen-sun-protection-factor

Team HomeServe. (2021). HomeServe. https://www.homeserve.com/en-us/blog/how-to/use-tape-to-hang-pictures

Thomas, L. (2023). Blackheads and whiteheads: Overview. News Medical Life Sciences. https://www.news-medical.net/health/Blackheads-and-Whiteheads-Overview.aspx

What is the KonMari method? (n.d). Konmari. https://konmari.com/about-the-konmari-method

What is tumble dry? (n.d). Whirlpool. https://www.whirlpool.com/blog/washers-and-dryers/what-is-tumble-dry.html

9 781961 326132